Bread for the Banquet

Experiencing Life in the Spirit

Kaleidoscope

Statement of Purpose

Kaleidoscope is a series of adult educational resources developed for the ecumenical church by Lancaster Theological Seminary and the United Church Board for Homeland Ministries. Developed for adults who want serious study and dialogue on contemporary issues of Christian faith and life, Kaleidoscope offers elective resources designed to provide new knowledge and new understanding for persons who seek personal growth and a deeper sense of social responsibility in their lives.

Kaleidoscope utilizes the expertise of professionals in various disciplines to develop study resources in both print and video. The series also provides tools to help persons develop skills in studying, reflecting, inquiring critically, and exploring avenues of appropriate Christian responses in life.

Kaleidoscope provides sound and tested resources in theology, biblical studies, ethics, and other related subjects that link personal growth and social responsibility to life situations in which adult Christian persons develop.

Bread for the Banquet

Experiencing Life in the Spirit

Elaine M. Ward

A Kaleidoscope Series Resource

United Church Press
New York

KALEIDOSCOPE SERIES

Scripture quotations from the Revised Standard Version of the Bible, copyrighted 1946, 1952, © 1971, 1973, by the Division of Christian Education of the National Churches of Christ in the United States of America, and are used by permission. In some instances adaptations have been made for the sake of inclusive language and clarity. Where noted as TEV, quotations are from the *Good News Bible: The Bible in Today's English Version*, copyright © 1966, 1971, 1976, by the American Bible Society, and are used by permission. Where noted as NEB, quotations are from *The New English Bible*, copyright © The Delegates of the Oxford University Press and the Syndics of the Cambridge University Press 1961, and are reprinted by permission. Permission is given in the Leader's Guide edition to reproduce only the author's discussion questions for group use.

Additional acknowledgement of permissions is found in the Notes section of this volume.

Library of Congress Cataloging-in-Publication Data

Ward, Elaine M.
   Bread for the banquet : experiencing life in the Spirit / Elaine M. Ward.
       p.   cm.   —(A Kaleidoscope series resource)
   Includes bibliographical references.
   ISBN 0–8298–0859–0.   —   ISBN 0–8298–0859–0 (leader's guide ed.)
   1. Spiritual life.   2. Spiritual exercises.   I. Title.
II. Series.
BV4501.2.W3355   1990
248—dc20
                                                        90-41011
                                                        CIP
                                                        Rev

United Church Press, 475 Riverside Drive, New York, N.Y. 10115

To

Nancy G. Wright
and
the Lancaster Theological Seminary Community

How to Use the Kaleidoscope Series

The Kaleidoscope book is the basic resource in the Kaleidoscope Series. For each Kaleidoscope book there is a Leader's Guide edition, which has a sixteen-page Leader's Guide bound into the back of the book. If this book is used for group study, the leader will need to study both the basic text and the Leader's Guide to prepare to lead study sessions. The video is a very helpful tool for the leader and the class when using this book as a study resource.

Contents

Introduction to the Kaleidoscope Series   ix

Preface   xi

1. Christian Spirituality   1

2. Biblical Spirituality   21

3. Religious Experience   44

4. The Story As Spiritual Guide   63

5. Creation Spirituality   85

6. Prophetic Spirituality   107

Notes   131

Bibliography   137

Introduction to the Kaleidoscope Series

Through direct experience, our faculty at Lancaster Theological Seminary discovered that a continual demand exists for Christian theological reflection upon issues of current interest. To meet this demand, the Seminary for many years has offered courses for lay people. To offer the substance of these courses to the wider Christian public is the purpose of the Kaleidoscope Series.

Lancaster Seminary exists to proclaim the gospel of Jesus Christ for the sake of the church and the world. In addition to preparing men and women for the ordained Christian ministry, the Seminary seeks to be a center of theological reflection for clergy and laity. Continuing education and leadership development for all Christians focus our mission. The topics and educational style in the Kaleidoscope Series extend Lancaster Seminary's commitment: theological study reflective of the interaction of the Bible, the world, the church, worship, and personal faith. We hope that this course will provide an opportunity for you to grow in self-understanding, in knowledge of other people and God's creation, and in the spirit of Christ.

We wish to thank the staff of the Division of Education and Publication of the United Church Board for Homeland Ministries for their support in this enterprise. The Rev. Dr. Ansley Coe Throckmorton, The Rev. Dr. Larry E. Kalp, and The Rev. Dr.

Percel O. Alston provided encouragement and support for the project. In particular, we are grateful for the inspiration of Percel Alston, who was a trustee of Lancaster Seminary. His life-long interest in adult education makes it most appropriate that this series be dedicated to him. Two other staff members have guided the series through the writing and production stages: The Rev. Willard Wetzel, Project Coordinator for the Kaleidoscope Series, and The Rev. Nancy G. Wright, Editor for Kaleidoscope. As a publishing staff they have provided valuable experience and counsel. Finally, I wish to recognize the creative leadership of Mrs. Jean Vieth, the Seminary Coordinator for the Series, who has been active for several years in this educational program at Lancaster.

Peter M. Schmiechen, President
The Lancaster Theological Seminary

Preface

You have prepared a banquet for me.
—Psalm 23:5, paraphrased

With eagerness and anticipation she closed her eyes, opened her hands in her lap with palms up, placed her feet flat on the floor, and took three long, deep breaths, breathing in and out slowly.

She tried to clear her mind, but other images invaded the empty space. She swept them away swiftly, and a dozen questions took their place to plague her. She shooed them out as well and rested again in stillness. Her mind was blank. The room, though filled with eleven other people, was silent. She wondered if they were meditating. She composed her grocery list without being aware that she was thinking. She worried about her children and about what she really wanted from life and what God wanted from her. Should she quit her job and risk a new future? "Where is God?" she asked. "Why me? If only . . . Oh, there you are," and again she remembered to rid her mind of thinking in order to be alone in solitude with God. It was only the first day of a five-day meditation retreat, and she was restless and unable to concentrate.

I was that eager, restless woman, and that retreat was nine years ago. The retreat began an even more intensive search for "bread for the banquet." Today I have tasted the nourishment of that bread. I write this with humility and hesitancy, remembering the story of the fourth-century Desert Father who, when a student came to him with questions that he had never before asked or taken seriously, the father replied, "You have not yet chosen your ship, nor put your baggage aboard, nor even packed your bags to cross the sea. How can you talk as if you had already arrived at the place you intend to go?"

I do not have all of the answers. I have not yet arrived where I intend to go, but I have "packed my bags" and "chosen my ship," and I invite you to go with me to God's banquet, to be with God, to eat the bread God offers us, and to share it with others.

All of us know from science and experience that muscles not used will stiffen. For many, the spiritual world, which can be experienced through meditation and prayer, dreams and visions, and in other ways has been disregarded or held suspect for so long that our awareness of it has atrophied.

Many of us become discouraged or unwilling to spend time in prayer. It is hard work to sit still in silence and solitude. We may feel an absence of God when we do so or may expect something dramatic to happen that does not. Some of us are afraid God may ask us to obey a command for which we are not ready. Or we may simply be unaware of the existence of the spiritual world—the living reality of the Holy Spirit within and among us. We may feel like the religious person in need of healing who is told that if she has enough faith she will be healed; when she remains disabled, she feels even more dis-ease.

I write this book for all who are hungry but who believe there is only one kind of bread, only one way of being with God. I believe that there are many gifts and many different ways to God and that God feeds us in a variety of ways. I write this book for you and me, for the times we feel alone, confused, hurt, or helpless. I write it as a reminder that in those "dark nights" we are not alone, that the amazing and unbelievable fact is that God is and that God is here now and that Jesus, a person, embodied God, a fact almost too good to be true.

Finding time for spiritual growth through praying, journal writing, listening to music, or walking in the presence of God transforms the quality of existence, infuses it with hope and meaning. Taking time for reflection is not selfishness but discovery of strength and inner resources we did not know existed. I write this as a storyteller, who has learned from stories that speak to the heart, and I write this as one in continuous amazement at the power of the Holy Spirit, the presence of Jesus, and the persuasive love of God on my pilgrimage. I invite you to "Come, eat bread at the banquet."

> For everything there is a season . . .
> A time to wait and a time to meditate,
> A time to read and a time to reflect,
> A time to dream and a time to write,
> A time to listen and a time to tell,
> A time for sound and sight and smell,
> A time to worship, and serve, and love—
> Always a time to love.

Chapter 1

Christian Spirituality

Lord, teach us to pray.
—Luke 11:1

When Kabezya-Mpungu, the highest god, created the sky and the earth, he made two human beings, man and woman, endowed with reason, for they did not yet possess Mutima, Heart. The great god also had four children: Sun, Rain, Moon, and Darkness; and he called them together to say that he would soon leave, so humans would no longer see his face, but he would send Mutima in his place. Not long after that Mutima, Heart, came along in a container no bigger than a hand, crying to Sun, Rain, Moon, and Darkness, "Where is Kabezya-Mpungu, our father?" They replied that they did not know, and Mutima said, "Oh, how great is my desire to commune with him, but since I cannot find him, I will enter man and woman, and through them I will seek God from generation to generation." And that is what happened. All children born of man and woman contain Mutima, a longing for God.

When I heard the late Jesuit storyteller Ken Feit tell this West African story many years ago, I recalled the words of Augustine, "Our hearts are restless until they rest in Thee, O God."

Living in a fragmented and frantic world, we hunger for wholeness, for *shālōm* (peace). We have a longing for God, for the bread, the spiritual food that will sustain and satisfy us; and God invites us to eat, providing us bread for the banquet. We are fed through prayer and meditation, scripture and story, music and movement, dreams and journalizing, and also through nature, worship, service, and love. Each of us, with our own hungers and tastes, comes into God's presence as we are. No matter how inadequate, awkward, or incomplete, we bring to God who we are. We pray as we can, for we know with Paul that "we do not know how to pray as we ought,

1

but the Spirit . . . intercedes for us with sighs too deep for words [Rom. 8:26]."

It is when we begin to pray that God shows each of us his or her own way. The author of the fourteenth-century spiritual classic *The Cloud of Unknowing* wrote: "If you ask me how you are to begin, I must pray Almighty God, of his grace and courtesy, to tell you himself. Indeed, it is good for you to realize that I cannot teach you. It is not to be wondered at. For this is the work of God alone, deliberately wrought in whatever soul he chooses, irrespective of the merits of that particular soul."[1]

"Behold, I stand at the door and knock [Rev. 3:20]," Christ said, and our longing unlocks the door to let God come in. We come into the presence of God through our longing.

Julian of Norwich, a fourteenth-century mystic, called that longing a "love-longing." "In every circumstance," she wrote in her long text, the reflections of twenty years on her sixteen revelations, "this presence [of God] is most desired, for it creates that wonderful security in true faith and certain hope."[2] Julian believed that to seek with faith and hope and love was very pleasing to God. Truly longing for God prepares us for God's presence. In some way it makes us worthy.

Six hundred years later Julian's compatriot C.S. Lewis discovered the same longing for God and named it "Joy." Lewis used the word to describe his desire, his longing, for union with the Absolute. He recognized that for him divine union was unattainable. Yet Lewis believed that the very presence of desire was its own fulfillment. Irreconcilable opposites (such as desire for permanent, felt union with God—an unfulfilled desire for mortals) could only be dealt with by living out the tension between them. The very nature of Joy makes nonsense of our common distinction between having and wanting.

I wonder if this is not the experience of most of us? My own longing for the Absolute began early in my life, but I did not experience that longing as "having." However, it is, perhaps, the sense of the absence of the Absolute that strengthens our search and our longing. And, paradoxically, when we experience God's presence, the longing for God becomes even more intense. "Having" enkindles in us even greater desire.

When we eat and are satisfied, we expect permanence. When

our inner life is fed, we sing and dance down the path of peace. We take for granted duration until we stumble and fall and the longing returns. There is no permanence. Life is ebb and flow, up and down, in and out.

Lewis was also aware of the danger of a greedy impatience to have what we desire. I recall that I hesitated in the beginning of my search for an intimate relationship with God through prayer and meditation because I feared manipulating God out of my deep longing.

Yet the Catholic twentieth-century monk and writer Thomas Merton reminds us in *What Is Contemplation?* that life in the spirit (contemplation) is the work of the Holy Spirit, a gift, a free gift of God given to all at baptism. He suggests that "God often measures His gifts by our desire to receive them, and by our cooperation with his grace."[3]

The desire, the longing, for God is our work. The fulfilling of that desire, however, is a gift. Life in the spirit is the work of the Holy Spirit, of Spirit calling to spirit and of God calling us to the banquet. We are not alone in our longing, however, for Christ longs in love to gather us all unto himself. Julian was sustained in her seeking because through the power of her longing, Christ enabled her to respond to that longing, which comes from God's everlasting goodness. "I am he who makes you long," she heard Christ say.[4]

An old Hasidic story, "The Flute," tells of a certain villager who used to pray on the Days of Awe in the House of Prayer of the Baal Shem Tov ("Master of the Good Name of God," their leader). His son, who could neither read nor write and was completely ignorant, had a flute on which he would play while watching his flock of sheep. His father never took him to the House of Prayer until the day he became Bar Mitzvah, and then he took him just to make sure he did not eat on the holy fast day. That day the boy sat through Yom Kippur without praying, because he did not know how. "Father," he whispered, "I want to play my flute." His father was aghast and shook his head to refuse the boy. During the Afternoon Prayer the boy asked again, and his father, of course, refused again, this time even holding the boy's pocket so he could not reach his flute. During the Closing Prayer, however, the boy forced the flute from his pocket and played a loud blast. When the

Baal Shem Tov heard the sound, he shortened his prayer, saying, "With the sound of his flute this child has lifted up all of our prayers. The flame of his longing kindled a fire within him and because of the strength of his longing, he played the song of his heart truly, for the sole sake of the Name of God."

God's Invitation to the Banquet of Life

We long to know God, to experience God's love in our lives, to live life in the Spirit. And God, the Host and Creator of life, invites us to the banquet, providing us with bread.

Bread is an important symbol for the Christian. It is a symbol of life and of our daily physical needs. God fed the Hebrews manna daily in the wilderness, and over and over we also read in scripture of God's feeding the people bread. In ancient times eating together was important, for the people believed that when two or three ate together, God was present. It was also a symbolic way of saying to the other diners, "You are my sister, my brother. I will take care of you."

Jesus told the story of "The Great Banquet" (see Luke 14:16–24): A certain man was preparing a great banquet and invited many guests. At the time of the banquet he sent his servant to tell those who had been invited, "Come, for everything is now ready." But they all alike began to make excuses. The first said, "I have just bought a field, and I must go and see it. Please excuse me." Another said, "I have just bought five yoke of oxen, and I'm on my way to try them out. Please excuse me." Still another said, "I just got married, so I can't come."

The servant came back and reported this to his master. Then the owner of the house became angry and ordered his servant, "Go out quickly into the streets and alleys of the town and bring in the poor, the crippled, the blind and the lame." "Sir," the servant said, "what you ordered has been done, but there is still room."

Then the master told his servant, "Go out to the roads and country lanes and make them come in, so that my house will be full. I tell you, not one of those who were invited will get a taste of my banquet."

There are many levels at which we hear a story, for stories are symbolic. Some explanation, however, is required for today's reader of Luke in order to understand the oriental concepts within Jesus' story. Nowadays, if we are invited to come to a banquet a year from today and accept, only extreme emergencies will keep us from attending. If we are invited for tomorrow, however, we will casually come or not, thinking our host had invited us at the last minute. But in Jesus' time, if a person were invited for a year from today, he or she would have no intention of going. If, on the other hand, a person accepted an invitation for the next day, he or she would be bound to attend, for before preparing a first-century banquet, the host would have to be assured that the guests were coming. If the host butchered a large animal, the guests had a moral obligation to help eat it, for in those days there was no refrigeration and the meat would spoil.

Let us look at the first excuse. "I have just bought a field and must go see it." To a Westerner such an excuse might seem feasible, but in the Middle East buying and selling land takes a great deal of time. There is not much land in the Middle East to sell. Therefore, it is quite valuable and takes months of study and survey. So to say, "I have bought a field and must go to see it" is a flimsy excuse. Consider the second excuse: "I have just bought five yoke of oxen, and I'm on my way to try them out. Please excuse me." In order to buy oxen to pull the plow, a person must go to the marketplace. Even today there is a stall and ground where a prospective buyer can hook up the oxen to a plow to try them out to determine their strength and obedience. The buyer will try different pairs together. To buy one pair would take a day, but to buy five pairs in one day is utterly ridiculous. In first-century Palestine the listeners would have seen this excuse as a joke.

Another invited guest said, "I just got married, so I can't come." Because oriental villages have from two hundred to a thousand people living in close quarters, one banquet at a time would be all that any one village could hold. It is impossible that two major events could take place at the same time. Even more important, however, is the fact that in an oriental culture a man does not discuss women in polite society. Women are a sacred topic, so to refuse a formal banquet, whose invitation the guest has already accepted, by rudely saying, "I have a woman in the back of the house and am busy" is an insult to the host.

So the master sends his servant to compel other people to come in. We see here how scripture is sometimes used to meet perceived human needs. For example, consider that the Spanish Inquisition was built on a misunderstanding of this verse: If people do not come, you have the right to force them. During the Inquisition the religious authorities tortured and killed those who refused to become Christian. What the story means, however, is that when a person is invited to a feast, that person is being accepted as a social equal. If you invite a peasant to sit with you, the Near Eastern culture requires that he or she refuse loudly in order to discover if you are sincere in your invitation. The outcasts, the dispossessed persons, must finally be all but dragged into the banquet hall in order to convince them of the host's welcome. The master says to the servant, "Do it! I am in earnest." The outcasts of Israel are invited to the banquet, for the poor have no other invitations, the maimed do not marry, the blind do not look for a field, and the lame do not buy oxen.

When I hear this story, I see an image of a large table. At one end of the table are, to our eyes, the misfits, the unfortunates, the marginal of society. Their table manners are atrocious. They aggressively tear and gnaw and loudly chew and belch their food. They are the poor, the homeless, the broken hearted, the dispossessed, the unloved. At the other end of the table, as far away as possible, are the rich, for they are shocked and offended by the grossness, the animal-like behavior of their fellow guests. They cannot imagine why the host invited the marginal group, who can never repay the invitation. In the middle, between the poor and the rich, sit the rest. Some of them look enviously at the end of the table where the rich sit and inch closer, as close as they are able to come in order to listen and look and pretend they are one of the rich. Some even hope that after this meal the outcasts at the other end will try harder. Others shake their heads. They are sorry for the poor, who hunger for physical bread, and for the rich, some of whom are deficient in love and spiritual nourishment. Finally, a small group even take their provisions to one end of the table to share, confident that they will eat again, or to the other end, knowing that all people need love; and still others move comfortably from one end of the table to the other, celebrating with both.

In Jesus' story, however, there were no rich nor even middle folk, for they had all made excuses not to attend. It reminds me of the story "Excuses."

"Why not?" was the first thing he said, when I refused. He had never seen me before. "Why not?" I knew that he had me. I brought up excuses. "My wife . . . the people I have to work with . . . not enough time . . . I guess it's my temperament." There was a sword hanging on the wall. He took it and gave it to me. "Here, with this sword, you can cut through any barriers." I took it and slipped away without saying a word. Back in my room in the guest house, I sat down and kept looking at that sword. I knew that what he said was true. But the next day I returned his sword. How can I live without my excuses?[5]

God invites us to the banquet, and we too may make excuses. Those who hear may realize that the kingdom is not "out there" but among us and that a person can only be fed by coming to the banquet. God's banquet is a symbol for wholeness. As Host, God invited all, but it was the wounded who came. The wounded are those of us who recognize our need and our longing, and we desire the bread God offers, in order to become whole.

God invites us to eat at his banquet, but no one can eat the bread for us, no one can experience God's love for us. A story goes that a rabbi who was well versed in the sacred writings was asked why he visited the zaddikim (leaders of the Jewish mystical movement Hasidism). What could they tell him that he could not learn from his books just as well? He answered the inquisitors, but they did not understand him. That evening they invited the rabbi to go to a play with them, but he refused. When they returned, they told him about the wonderful things they had seen. "I know all about those wonderful things," he said. "I have read the program." They protested, saying, "You cannot possibly know what we have just seen with our own eyes." "Yes," agreed the rabbi. "That is just how it is with the books and the zaddikim."[6]

Jesus, the Bread of Life

And when almighty God looked out at the people he had
created, he saw that they lacked bread. And God became incarnate
in the form of their need. And Jesus said, "I am the bread of life."

Jesus knew the importance of food. He ate with his friends. He
fed the people. He even commanded his disciples to feed his sheep.
He even stated that feeding the hungry is one of his criteria for
entering God's realm: "for I was hungry and you gave me something to eat [author's paraphrase; see Matthew 25:35]."

In the story found in John 6:25–35, Jesus had fed the multitudes
with bread. The next day they looked for him, and when they
found him, they asked, "When did you get here?" Jesus replied, "I
am telling you the truth: you are looking for me because you ate
the bread and had all you wanted, not because you understood my
miracles [TEV]."

Jesus did not answer the question, for he was not interested in
rational, logical, factual answers and definitions. Jesus was interested in life in the Spirit. "Do not work for food that spoils, but for
food that endures to eternal life," he said, "food which the Son of
Man will give you." Jesus' actions as well as his words showed his
spiritual attitude toward life. He cried in public. He blessed and
coddled children and used them as examples for adults to follow.
He was aware of birds and flowers and appreciated their beauty, and
he gave gentle answers to threatening questions, as he told stories
of hope and of God's love. He admitted to being hungry or tired,
sad or happy. Also, he was a man of feeling and was hurt by people
and by evil and by injustice. Jesus showed compassion and care for
the disabled: the lame, the blind, the paralyzed, the dispossessed,
the poor, the hungry, and the hurt. He overturns the image of our
modern establishment's culture with its aggressive, competitive,
materialistic standards, for Jesus did not possess nor compete.
Instead, he turned people's values and visions upside down, inside
out. "Blessed are the poor . . . the meek," he said. This Jesus feeds
us as the bread of our lives and gives us permission to be sensitive,
vulnerable, and tender. He even commands it: "Unless you change
and become like little children [open, dependent, vulnerable,
helpless], you will not enter the realm of God [Matt. 18:3,
paraphrased]."

Jesus, in his compassion, knowing the unity of the body and the spirit, fed the people both physical and spiritual food. The tempter, too, as recorded in Matthew 4, knew the deep connection between the body and spirit and the people's need for nourishment. When he invited Jesus, "If you are the Son of God, tell these stones to become bread," he indicated that Jesus could win the loyalty and love of the people if he would feed them. So Jesus does in a special way, later promising that "anyone who eats and drinks of me will hunger and thirst no more." But to the tempter's words he quoted scripture, knowing the terrible power of the temptation; he said, "The scripture says, 'One cannot live on bread alone, but on every word that God speaks [Matt. 4:4, TEV].'" Jesus as the Word of God is the Bread that nourishes and satisfies us.

In her tenth revelation Julian of Norwich saw Jesus as we would see him today in contemporary pictures of the Sacred Heart, but in Julian's vision there is no morbidity. Jesus is not the Man of Sorrows but the glorified Christ. In chapter 51 of her *Showings* she wrote that "our courteous Lord revealed a wonderful example of a lord who has a servant, and gave me sight for the understanding of them both."[7] She then tells the story of the servant who stood before his lord ready to do his will. When he was given the lord's instructions, he dashed off at great speed and soon fell into a pit and was injured. In great pain the servant groaned and moaned but could not rise to help himself in any way. But the greatest hurt was his lack of consolation, for he could not turn his face to look on his loving lord, in whom is all consolation. But the lord said to Julian that he would reward his beloved servant for his fright and fear, hurt and injuries, and for all his woe.

This revelation was given as an answer to Julian's prayer. Because she at first did not fully understand, she meditated on the revelation for twenty years, then wrote in her long text: "I understood that the servant before him [God] was Adam . . . injured in his powers and made most feeble. . . . And then I saw that only pain blames and punishes, and our courteous Lord comforts and succors, and always he is kindly disposed to the soul, loving and longing to bring us to his bliss." The servant also was the second person of the Trinity, and included Adam, that is to say, all persons. Julian saw Christ taking "our foul mortal flesh, Adam's old tunic, tight-fitting, threadbare, and short, made lovely, new, white, bright and forever clean by God's Son."[8]

So Jesus comes to us as bread, to feed and comfort us, and through our needs and longings to reveal to us his presence, for it is not dogmas nor doctrines that comfort us in crises but the Incarnation who loves us. The author of *Epistle of Privy Counsel,* claimed to be the same fourteenth-century author of *The Cloud of Unknowing,* wrote, "This is what the perfect lover does: he completely strips himself for the sake of the one he loves, nor will he allow himself to be clothed in anything except in that which he loves: not only for a while, but for ever to be absorbed in it, himself fully and finally forgotten. This is the work of love that none may know but the one who experiences it. The Lord says, 'I am the boundless raiment of love through all eternity and for ever'."[9]

This is the work of love, but sometimes we become careless. The Desert Fathers tell the story (I shall call it "Careless") of Abba Elias who said:

"An old man was living in a temple and the demon came to say to him, 'Leave this place which belongs to us,' and the old man said, 'No place belongs to you.' Then they began to scatter his palm leaves about, one by one, and the old man went on gathering them together with persistence. A little later the devil took his hand and pulled him to the door. When the old man reached the door, he seized the lintel with the other hand crying out, 'Jesus, save me.' Immediately the devil fled away. Then the old man began to weep. The Lord said to him, 'Why are you weeping?' and the old man said, 'Because the devils have dared to seize a man and treat him like this.' The Lord said to him, 'You had been careless. As soon as you turned to me again, you see I was beside you.'"[10]

The biggest problem for men and women today, and even for the Desert Father, the wise old man, is the temptation to control instead of to trust. Yet over and over, when my spirit is weary or hurt or full of love-longing, I hear Jesus say through this story, "But you did not ask me."

In the story of the feeding of the multitudes, the people asked Jesus, "What must we do to do the works God requires?" and Jesus answered, "The work of God is this: to believe in the one he has sent [John 6:28–29, paraphrased]." We do not work for the bread. The bread is given us. Our task is to accept and believe. And they said to him, "Lord, give us this bread always."

Come, the banquet is ready.

Christian Spirituality as "Being with God"

Three fathers used to go to visit blessed Anthony every year, and two of them used to discuss their thoughts and the salvation of their souls with him; but the third always remained silent and did not ask him anything. After a long time, Abba Anthony said to him: "You often come here to see me, but you never ask me anything," and the other replied, "It is enough to be with you, Father."[11]

Christian spirituality is being with God, seeking and experiencing God as dynamic, living, and loving. It is less *knowing about* God and more *being with* God. It is experiencing the Spirit rather than explaining the Spirit. In a sense it is a homecoming, a coming home to the heart of God as the prodigal child, and there seeing and knowing and enjoying being with the Parent as if for the first time. Nothing is changed, and everything is changed.

The word *God* is a symbol for the reality we know more deeply than we know ourselves, and yet God is always more than and different from what we think and feel about God, for God is Spirit, Absolute Transcendence here and now, among us and within us. That which is holy is beyond our knowing in a rational way. Only in story can we express the mystery and majesty of God. The Hindu story "The Fig Tree and the Seed" is such a story:

A boy became the student of a wise teacher and studied and read many deep books about God and the world. He knew long prayers by heart and was proud of his learning. At last his father became aware that his son had become conceited by his knowledge, and so one day he asked his son, "How does life come from that which cannot be seen?" "I do not know," the boy admitted. "Bring me a fig from the fig tree," said his father. "Open it. What do you see?" "I see small seeds," his son replied. His father told him to cut open one of the seeds. "Now what do you see?" "Nothing," said the boy, wondering about the meaning of his father's questions. "You mean the tree grew from something you cannot see and that which is alive, that made the tree grow, cannot be seen?" "It must be so," said the son. "That is true for all of life. Nothing in the world could have been without that invisible and living part from which it came. The invisible is God. God gave you life. God is your life. We are all one." The son saw what his father was doing, and he became interested. "Help me understand more," he begged. His father showed him some salt and told him to place it in a glass of water, and the son did as his father said. Then his father asked him for the salt. "I do not see it anymore," the son said. The father told his son to taste the water, and the water tasted salty; yet no salt could be seen. "Although your eyes do not see God, there are other ways you can know God is everywhere. As the salt, God is hidden. God is Spirit, all that which is really true."[12]

Christianity is more than a belief. It is an experience. The heart of the Christian faith is communion with God, life in the Spirit. Rather than describing God and religion as objects of belief, which is the role of theology, Christian spirituality is reaction and response from a personal participation in the mystery of Christ through prayer and meditation.

Augustine (bishop 396–430) looked for God everywhere and found God in his heart. "Return to your heart," Augustine said, "and find God." Christian spirituality is a spirituality of the heart. We learn to know God by loving God, but learning and knowing are not the same thing. When an eminent Talmudic authority, hearing of a famous prodigy at a Talmudic college in Poland, asked the head of the institution, "Is it true what I have heard of his marvelous store of knowledge?" the rabbi replied with a smile, "To tell you the truth, the young fellow studies so much I do not know where he can find time to know!"

Christian spirituality is the attempt to be whole in body and spirit, mind and heart. It involves listening to the warbler, dancing one's doctrines and creeds, singing one's faith, feeling and committing one's life, and professing one's longings and loves. We are led to learn new skills and knowledge to bring our own uniqueness to fulfillment and expression. To give expression to the Spirit is to have direct contact with living, spiritual reality. We then give shape to what we believe and feel and know, to enable others to feed on the sustaining food of life.

There is another story, probably familiar, that tells of a stranger approaching a woman at the well on the outskirts of her village. When he asked what the village ahead was like, she asked him what the village was like that he had just left. The man described his irritation with the unfriendliness of the people, the scarcity of entertainment, and the poverty of beauty. She replied that the town ahead was the same, and the man returned to the place from which he had come without visiting the village. Later, another stranger asked the woman the same question; she repeated her inquiry. He spoke of the friendliness of the people he had left, the fullness of things to do, and the beauty of the scenery. She replied, "The village ahead is the same."

How we think affects what we see. Christian spirituality is a way of seeing and being in the world. It is a faith stance, an attitude toward all of life. But Christian spirituality cannot be taught. Facts outside ourselves can be taught and talked about. There is a body of knowledge in the physical world that experts can convey. But inside facts—those which we feel and intuit, those truths about our oneness with God and the world—are aspects of the spiritual world.

The Power of Prayer

"What is the chief end of a person?" is the first question in John Calvin's Genevan Catechism. "To know God and enjoy God forever" is the answer. Prayer is the way to know and enjoy God forever.

A rabbi told the following story: "People come to me who ride to market every day of the week. One such man approached me and cried: 'My dear rabbi! I haven't gotten anything out of life. All week I get out of one wagon and into another. But when a man stops to think that he is permitted to pray to God himself, he lacks nothing at all in the world.'" [13]

This is like a man who came to a woman of faith and told her, "I pray but I have no sense of being close to God." And she replied, "The only way is through love, the giving of love. Love more and you will be closer to God. Love less and you will be further from God. Choose life and you will grow closer to God. Empty yourself and receive from God."

Although there is power in prayer, we work and pray, think and pray, trust and pray, suffer and pray. Prayer is not a lazy substitute for work and thought. A flat tire is not inflated by praying over it. The power of prayer is learning to know how deeply we are loved by God; such knowledge gives us freedom from what blocks us from living fully: fear, fanaticism, doubt, despair, selfishness, and separation from others; for freedom from fear is the freedom to love.

Richard J. Foster in *Celebration of Discipline* tells of a friend who taught emotionally handicapped children and decided to pray for them. He did not tell the children of his prayers. He simply prayed. When one of the children would crawl under his desk and take a fetal position, he would take the child in his arms and pray silently that the light of Christ would heal the hurt within the child. Soon the child would relax and return to his desk. By the end of the school year, every child but two was able to return to a regular classroom. [14]

I agree with William James when he wrote, "Through prayer, religion insists, things which cannot be realized in any other manner come about: energy which but for prayer would be bound is by prayer set free and operates in some part, be it objective or subjective, in the world of facts." [15] There is real power in prayer, though we are not always able to define or articulate it.

Meditation in Silence and Solitude

When you pray, go into your room, close the door and pray to your Father, who is unseen. Then your Father, who sees what is done in secret, will reward you. And when you pray, do not keep on babbling like pagans, for they think they will be heard because of their many words. Do not be like them, for your Father knows what you need before you ask him.

—Matthew 6:6–8, paraphrased

Be still and know that I am God.
—I Kings 19:12

Some brothers . . . went to see Abba Felix, and they begged him to say a word to them. But the old man kept silent. After they had asked for a long time he said to them, "You wish to hear a word?" They said, "Yes, Abba." Then the old man said to them, "There are no more words nowadays. When the brothers used to consult the old men and when they did what was said to them, God showed them how to speak. But now, since they ask without doing that which they hear, God has withdrawn the grace of the word from the old men, and they do not find anything to say, since there are no longer any who carry their words out." Hearing this, the brothers groaned, saying, "Pray for us, Abba."[16]

Perhaps the most meaningful thing to say about God is to keep silent in the presence of the Spirit. Silence is not the absence of God, but the very presence of God, for silence is pregnant with possibility. God waits for us in the silence, but silence can be such an awkward thing. Studies show how uncomfortable teachers are with silence. After they ask a question of their students, the waiting time for an answer is less than one minute; and when there is no response, teachers answer their own question or move on to a new one.

The first year that I taught five-day kindergarten in the church, I feared what young children might do with silence; so after each morning's daily prayer, I quickly moved on to something else. One morning at the close of the prayer, Debbie spoke out: "Mrs. Ward, you always end just as I begin!"

Maria Ranier Rilke wrote a small book about silence and trust, *Letters to a Young Poet*, in which he admitted his own love and hate for silence and solitude, the foundation for all genuine work. "Go into yourself and test the deeps in which your life takes rise," he wrote. ". . . Take whatever comes with great trust."[17]

In silence we experience loneliness. Everyone experiences loneliness at one time or another. It creeps up on us unexpectedly, in a crowd of people, or during a holiday, or when it seems that no one listens or cares. We have called one too many times without a mutual exchange; and when we do talk, the heart of the matter is absent and we feel empty and sad. Loneliness is no respecter of people, young or old.

After working fourteen hours a day, a clergyman came to the
famous psychologist Carl Jung, his nerves in shambles, his hands
shaking. The good doctor prescribed working eight hours a day,
sleeping eight hours, and spending the remaining hours alone in
his study in quiet. Easy advice and inexpensive enough to follow,
the minister agreed. After two days he returned to Dr. Jung,
complaining that it had not worked. "What did you do?" Jung
asked.

The patient told him that after supper he went to his study,
played a few Chopin Études, and finished a Hermann Hesse novel.
The next day he did the same, only reading Thomas Mann's *Magic
Mountain* and playing a Mozart sonata.

> "But you did not understand," Jung replied. "I did not want
> you with Hermann Hesse or Thomas Mann or even Mozart or
> Chopin. I wanted you to be all alone with yourself."
> At this point the minister looked terrified and gasped, "Oh,
> but I can't think of any worse company!" To this Dr. Jung made
> the reply that has been repeated so often: "And yet this is the
> self you inflict on other people fourteen hours a day."[18]

All too often at the bottom of our loneliness is a sense of
ourselves as unworthy company, but in God's company there is
unconditional love. In the presence of God we are wonderfully
loved, and growth and transformation come through a personal,
loving relationship with God. In prayer we open ourselves to God
and share our hopes and fears, loves and hates, hungers and hurts,
sorrows and joys; and the incredible mystery of it all is that it
becomes a mutual sharing. Made in the image of God, we love as
we are loved.

Mysticism

> *Oh, taste and see that the* Lord *is good!*
> —Psalm 34:8

> *I heard this from my grandfather: Once a fiddler played so sweetly
> that all who heard him began to dance, and whoever came near
> enough to hear, joined in the dance. Then a deaf man, who knew*

nothing of music, happened along, and to him all he saw seemed the action of madmen—senseless and in bad taste. [19]

Mysticism actually defies expression because it is an experience that ranges in images, words, and feelings, from the vague to the specific. It is experience rather than knowledge or concepts, for the mystic believes that knowledge about a thing is not the thing itself; therefore, critics of mysticism, or prayer, are merely swatting invisible flies.

I must admit that I am comfortable with ambiguity, paradox, and both/and responses and recognize that others live more "securely" with knowledge. It is not my intention to be indecisive or uncommitted over the questions, Is God immanent or transcendent? Is God immanent for some and transcendent for others? or Do we make that decision on the basis of our temperament? I believe in a God (the name, or metaphor we give to the One who is the Source, Author, Creator, Father, Mother, etc. of all life and meaning) big enough, mysterious enough, Beyond and Within enough to sustain all our faithful fumblings and vivid visions—or perhaps, since all good things come from God, not only to sustain but to *give* them. We hold in balance the intimacy and ultimacy of God, utter immanence and utter transcendence. The Transcendent Light and the Inward Love complement each other, and when they are taken together they define God.

Mysticism affirms that the human being is essentially divine and thus capable of immediate communion with God. It denies that knowledge is limited to the physical, visible reality. But though the mystic knows God through firsthand experience, that knowledge cannot be reasoned about.

Mysticism is concerned with loving God, with shifting the center of interest from self on the natural plane to union with God on the spiritual one, and with looking at all of life through that love. The mystic sings with the psalmist, "Oh, taste and see!" eat and be satisfied. The inner process of the mystic's experience includes the phases of spiritual growth, sometimes identified by spiritual writers as awakening, purgation, illumination, the "dark night of the soul," and union with God.

1. Awakening is a recognition of one's intense love for God and certitude of God's expression of love. It is the sense of the nearness

of God and the freedom of letting go in order to trust God. With this awareness comes the realization of finiteness and the need for self-surrender, an inner purification through love.

2. Purification, or purgation, is the pruning and training (the spiritual discipline) of the human spirit, which is the essence of all education. It is concerned with becoming detached from enslavement to the things of the senses, allowing the mystic entrance into the state of illumination.

The mystic on journey toward union with God surrenders to a self-denying and strict self-discipline, renouncing the comforts of society for poverty, chastity, and obedience. Poverty involves a detachment from all finite things. The vow of chastity is taken in order to cleanse the soul from personal desire; and obedience is complete self-abandonment. The mystics varied in what they gave up. Whatever impeded their growth toward union with God was to be discarded. Francis of Assisi loved lovely things. Therefore, he had to force himself to visit the lepers, whose sight and smell disgusted him. He learned, however, not only to serve them but to kiss them, and in so doing the sight and touch of lepers changed into sweetness. What begins as discipline becomes an act of love.

3. Illumination is experience of the sense of the Divine Presence, accompanied by a deep, intuitive knowledge of some of the secrets of God. Many mystics never go beyond this stage, but those longing for union with God willingly undertake further pursuit and with it the "dark night of the soul."

4. The "dark night of the soul" is a sense of divine absence, the sense of being abandoned by God. It ultimately leads to union with God.

5. Union with God is a state of peace and harmony, joy and enhanced power in the oneness of the All. It is an intensification of life, rather than a suppression of it; the paradox is that of surrendering oneself in order to own oneself. In this way one knows the love in which life in the Spirit is bathed. A new center is substituted for the ego, and the mystic now lives in oneness with the life of God.

A description of mysticism and the spiritual life is not complete without a brief sketch of six important spiritual traditions:

The Desert Fathers and Mothers. In the fourth century groups of men and women moved into the deserts of Egypt and Syria in order to renounce the life of the world. It was the desert that provided them the silence and solitude they needed to concentrate on and contemplate God alone. Here they could "pray constantly [1 Thess. 5:17]," and as temples of the Holy Spirit (1 Corinthians 3:16) they subjected themselves to austere discipline (ascesis). They strove to reach the state of integration of body, soul, and spirit in *hesychia* (rest, or tranquility), to meet and surrender to God by putting the mind in the heart as they prayed.

The Eastern Orthodox Tradition. Hesychasm, the distinctive spirituality of the Eastern Orthodox tradition, is based on the Jesus Prayer (the words of the prayer are, "Lord, Jesus Christ, have mercy on me, a sinner") prayed thousands of times daily as a way to contemplation and unification. The early church father Origen said that the spirit is deified by that which it contemplates. Gregory of Nyssa (Eastern church father, 335–394) wrote that God has made us not simply spectators of God's powers but participants in God's very nature. Yet God is unknowable, and knowledge of God is only available through the process of "unknowing," or renunciation of the use of the mind and senses through contemplation.

Monastic Spirituality. Monastic spirituality grew up in the West, centering on the recitation of the Divine Office of Prayer morning and evening, with the use of the Psalms as the book of prayer. As the Israelites were fed with manna by God in the wilderness, so the psalms were the "bread in the wilderness" for the monks.

Fourteenth-Century Mystic Spirituality. Some of the great names in the history of Christian spirituality are found in the fourteenth century. Such persons as Dante, Meister Eckhart, John Tauler, Henry Suso, John Ruysbroeck, Thomas à Kempis, Richard Rolle, the unknown author of *The Cloud of Unknowing,* Walter Hilton, Julian of Norwich, and Catherine of Siena lived in that period and wrote of their prayer experiences.

Counter-Reformation Spirituality. The number of spiritual classics from this period (sixteenth century) is vast. Three of the giants were Teresa of Avila, John of the Cross, and Ignatius of Loyola. All three became saints of the church.

Teresa, through her extraordinarily developed spiritual perceptions, pictured the Trinity as (a) God, Father-Creation, pure transcendent Being, creative source and origin of all that is; (b)

God, the Son, Christ, Logos or creative Word, bridge between the finite and the infinite; and (c) Holy Spirit of Divine Love, indwelling source of human spiritual consciousness, and link with the being of God. All three aspects she saw fused into one. Teresa was the author of a number of spiritual classics, including *The Interior Castle* and an autobiography, *The Book of Her Life.*

John of the Cross, author of *The Dark Night of the Soul* and other important works, identified the stage of the "dark night" in the mystic life. Both Teresa and John were members of the Carmelite order, and both advised against the preoccupation with the intellect in prayer. Teresa wrote, "It is not a matter of thinking a great deal but of loving a great deal—so do whatever arouses you most to love."[20]

Ignatius of Loyola, the great Catholic reformer, established the Jesuit order. He wrote in his *Spiritual Exercises,* "Our Father wanted us, in all our activities, as far as possible, to be free, at ease in ourselves, and obedient to the light given particularly to each one."[21] He provided techniques and aids to prayer, based on the importance of the imagination and participation in the biblical story.

Holiness, or Pentecostal, Spirituality. With their beginnings in the early twentieth century, the Holiness/Pentecostal groups stress speaking in tongues and healing, the experience of the Spirit's presence, and prayer. Prayer is central to all Pentecostal movements. (For a fuller development, see Kenneth Leech's *Soul Friend.*[22])

Since liberal Protestantism has tended to be ignorant of spiritual consciousness, or ignored its influence, a discussion of mysticism deserves more time than the space here allowed. Therefore, I recommend that beyond the compass of this chapter you begin a more extensive study by using the bibliography.

Chapter 2

Biblical Spirituality

Thy word is a lamp unto my feet.
—Psalm 119:105

I cut my teeth, as the saying goes, on the Bible. For as long as I can remember its stories perplexed me. They were indeed beyond belief. Yet as a child I accepted what adults told me about them. As I grew older, I listened to more learned folk tell me what the stories meant, why and in what context they were written. The stories were in my head, and they stayed there.

Then one day, seemingly out of the air, the foundations of my world shook, the pieces of my life that I had so carefully put together scattered, and I landed in the pit. I believe all of us have had experiences that require climbing out of the pit, or, again metaphorically, learning to swim when drowning. We then cry for help!

During this time, which extended over several years, my dreams were of drowning, of crying for help and of hearing the words: "I taught you to swim." These are the times when we forget all we know of swimming, when we are too confused to try to swim. We are like the lame man who needed four friends to carry him to Jesus until he was healed enough to walk for himself. In my pit-like situation I came to the healer. "Why are you here?" he asked. "I feel as if I have a wet dishrag inside and I want a hard avocado seed instead," I answered.

I talked. I walked. I read. Yes, I read, for reading had supported me all my life. But I could not read the Bible. I was angry at God. Poor God! But God can take our anger, and our pain, and our disease and transform, redeem them; and God fed and healed me through the Bible.

I heard the old story yet one more time, but this time it slipped

21

down from my head into my heart. Jesus asked *me*, "Do you want to be well?"

"But . . ."

"Get up, pick up your mat, and walk."

The Bible is God's food for the spirit. I "eat" its words today as bread at the banquet, for I know that no other food satisfies my hunger.

The theme of this book is that bread is a symbol of life and of our daily physical needs. Bread was a basic necessity in the life of biblical persons. The story of Israel's escape from bondage in Egypt and their wandering in the wilderness includes the story of God feeding them with physical bread. We, too, are fed in a variety of ways at God's banquet. One of the ways we are fed is by the hearing and the reading of God's holy word. Scripture is the bread we taste at the banquet. Reading, and reflecting upon, and reentering into these biblical stories are ways of coming closer to God. They lead to a spiritual knowing of God, in the heart as well as in the head, for symbol, metaphor, and poetry make meaning for the heart that we can taste and experience.

The heart of Christian spirituality lies in the absolutely unique influence of Jesus' words and personality. The divergent Gospels of the four evangelists present the rich impact made upon those who heard Jesus, the Word of God made flesh, speak. For he presents a new law, the transcending of all law through love. He makes possible the relation of God with human beings that ushers in the realm of God as actuality, a new creation.

Jesus' words are beyond belief. The story of Noah building a boat inland without a cloud in the sky, obeying God's command, is beyond belief. The story of Abraham hearing God's voice and leaving his home to cross a wilderness to begin a new people is beyond belief. The story of Moses standing before the burning bush and hearing God's voice is beyond belief. The stories of crossing the Red Sea on dry land, of great power and strength residing in the length of a person's hair, of living with lions and staying alive in a furnace of fire—all are beyond belief. Scripture can take us "beyond belief" to God, for although primacy belongs to scripture, ultimacy belongs to God. We are fed in order to praise and to feed.

The Bible is the story of God acting in the lives of a people, a community, and of their responses to these acts, acts in which they see God as the source and center of their inner and outer worlds. It is this story by which Christians learn and decide who they are and commit what they will do. At the heart of the Christian faith is the story that shapes, expresses, and transforms our sense of the world. The sacred word refreshes our spirit.

In *The Greek Passion* by Nikos Kazantzakis, Manolios is chosen to play the role of Christ in the passion play in his Greek village. The part absorbs him. Manolios goes to look for the priest Fotis to ask his aid, thinking that he, too, perhaps may have once passed through the same distress and be able to help him. The priest is away on his rounds of the neighboring villages to collect alms, so Manolios returns to his solitude and begins to read one of the Gospels for an answer. Kazantzakis wrote: "He opened the little book, as on the days of great heat people open wide a door giving on the sea. He plunged into the sacred text and was refreshed; he forgot the questions stabbing at him. His spirit no longer questioned; his heart was overflowing with response."[1]

We forget our questions as we encounter the Bible, which contains a story beyond belief, a story of trust that gives certainty to existence. Its sacred stories tell of God feeding with physical and spiritual bread.

God and Physical Bread

> *"Come, all you who are thirsty, come to the waters;*
> *and you who have no money, come, buy wine*
> *and milk without money and without cost."*
> —Isaiah 55:1

It was bread that brought together the family of Joseph (Genesis 43). And it is the memory of God's feedings and the sacred stories that we share together that feed us today.

The people gathered what they could eat daily, and on the sixth day twice as much for the sabbath, for the people rested on the seventh day, and the house of Israel called its name manna; it was like coriander seed, white, and the taste of it was like wafers made with honey. And Moses said, "This is what the

Lord has commanded: 'Let an omer of it be kept throughout your generations, that they may see the bread with which I fed you in the wilderness, when I brought you out of the land of Egypt.' "

—Exodus 16:22–32, paraphrased

In Joel we read of the invasion of the locusts and the lamentation over the ruin of the country, of the Israelites' need for bread (1:1–12) and of the call, therefore, to repentance and prayer (1:13–2:17). The Lord's answer is to send them grain, new wine and oil, and abundant showers. "You will have plenty to eat, until you are full [2:26, paraphrased]." And God promises yet even more: "And afterward, I will pour out my Spirit on all people [2:28, paraphrased]."

Over and over we are reminded of God's feeding with physical bread. And scripture, with its sacred stories, becomes our omer to remind us of that bread, for we rely more on narrative than on theory in our spiritual pilgrimage.

Physical and Spiritual Food for Elijah

Ahab became king of Israel and reigned in Samaria over Israel twenty-two years. He did "more evil in the eyes of the Lord than any of those before him," married Jezebel, and served and worshiped Baal. He even set up an altar for Baal in the temple of Baal that he built in Samaria. So Elijah the Tishbite said to Ahab, "As the LORD, the God of Israel, lives, whom I serve, there will be neither dew nor rain in the next few years except at my word [1 Kings 17:1, paraphrased]." (The story of Elijah is found in 1 Kings 16:29—19:8.)

Then the word of the Lord came to Elijah, telling him to leave and hide in the ravine of Kerith, and the ravens brought him bread and meat in the morning and in the evening, and he drank from the brook. When the brook dried up, God sent him to the widow at Zarephath, who fed him until the day the Lord gave rain on the land. But the story is not ended. After contesting with the prophets of Baal on Mount Carmel, Elijah had to run for his life. He ran into the desert, and when he came to a broom tree, he sat down under it and prayed that he might die. Then he lay down under the tree and fell asleep. All at once an angel touched him and said, "Get up and eat." He looked around, and there by his head was a cake of bread and a jar of water. He ate and drank and then lay down again. The angel of the Lord came back a second time and touched him and said, "Get up and eat, for the journey is too much for you." Elijah got up and ate and drank and, strengthened by that food, he traveled forty days and forty nights until he reached Horeb, the mountain of God. God fed Elijah with physical and with spiritual food for his journey. How often we come to the end of our day's journey to sit under the broom tree and ask, as Elijah, that we might die. "Take away my life," we moan. But when we lie down to sleep, the angel comes and says, "Arise and eat."

We eat, but our hungers are not filled once and for all. The angel reminds us that the journey will be too great. We cannot survive without food, physical food of bread and water, and spiritual food of God's Spirit. Times of crises, loss, and transition are periods in the wilderness where the angel comes and tells us to eat again and again. When we eat and are satisfied, we expect permanency. Now that our inner resources are fed, we sing and dance down the path. In that peace and happiness we take for granted duration, until we stumble and fall, and the hunger returns, and the angel again reminds us to arise and eat.

There is no permanency. In the tension of impermanency, however, is energy, growth and harmony, death and rebirth. God is there. Obeying our own inner laws, we move through cycles of risings and dyings, whose meaning is not permanent annihilation but dying with the possibility of rebirth into new life. We rise to eat again and again, and in that new life we renounce former illusions and attachments and desires that cause our disease and disharmony.

Jesus' Feeding of the People

Jesus knew the importance of physical bread. He taught his friends to pray, "Give us this day our daily bread." When he raised the daughter of Jairus from the dead, he said, "Give her something to eat [Luke 8:55, paraphrased]!" He said to the woman who begged him to drive the demon out of her daughter, "First let the children eat all they want, for it is not right to take the children's bread and toss it to the dogs." "Yes, Lord," she replied, "but even the dogs under the table eat the children's crumbs." Then he told her, "For such a reply, you may go; the demon has left your daughter [Mark 7:24–30, paraphrased]." And Jesus told his friends, "With desire I have desired to eat this passover with you [Luke 22:15, paraphrased]."

Jesus had compassion on the people, because they had been with him for three days and had not eaten; and they would collapse on the way home, for some had come from a long distance. When five loaves and two fish were brought to him, he gave thanks and broke them, and his friends fed the people. When they ate and were satisfied, the disciples gathered up twelve basketfuls of the pieces left over. In the story that follows Jesus walks on water; yet "the disciples were completely amazed, because they had not understood the real meaning of the feeding of the five thousand; their minds could not grasp it [Mark 6:52, TEV]."

Wisdom is different from understanding, and wisdom cannot be taught or communicated. Wisdom is understanding with the heart, seeing on a higher level of consciousness, where all is connected and lawfully related. Truth waits for eyes unclouded with confused desire.

The disciples thought only of physical bread, how their bodies would be fed, but Jesus was speaking not only of physical bread but of spiritual bread as well. Jesus said, "Are your hearts hardened?" When hearts are hardened, they are cut off from that which feeds them and they become very hungry.

Because of the size of the crowd in such a tiny country, because we are introduced to a person who shares, and because the modern mind cannot understand miracles, we have missed the significance of the story of the feeding of the five thousand. John wrote of Jesus' miracles of feeding and healing as signs that we might know that Jesus is the Christ, the bread of God.

Because we live in a day when the world is well aware of the hungry, we preach and teach the story as impressing upon us the importance of sharing. Well we might, in a world in such dire need of sharing. We have been taught that faith without works is dead, so we continue to preach sharing, for this is the message of the good news of the gospel. But the message of the Gospels is that God is the source of our food, both physical and spiritual. With John we affirm that Jesus supplies the food of life, the means of eternal life. John wrote that Jesus' asking how the people would be fed was a test, for "he himself already knew what he would do [John 6:6]."

"What food do you have?" Jesus asked, and we are asked to reply. Life in the Spirit is that of giving and receiving, eating and sharing.

God's Spiritual Food

In John we read: "Do not work for food that spoils, but for food that endures to eternal life, which the Son of man will give you [John 6:27]." And later he wrote: "Our fathers ate the manna in the desert; as it is written: 'He gave them bread from heaven to eat.'" Jesus said, "It is my Father who gives you the true bread from heaven. For the bread of God is he who comes down from heaven and gives life to the world." "Sir," they said, "from now on give us this bread." Then Jesus declared, "I am the bread of life. He who comes to me will never go hungry, and he who believes in me will never be thirsty [John 6:31–35, paraphrased]."

The Bible has always been food for the spirit. The Egyptian monks memorized whole books of the Bible, and the Desert Father Anthony, who had never learned to read, learned by heart the word of God for the purpose of meditation, of feeding the mind and heart.

We eat God's bread the first time to heal our despair. The second time, to provide strength for the journey and nourishment for the spirit on the inner journey. We discover our need for inner guidance and strength, for spiritual nurture during times of transition, of crises, when we are challenged to grow. These times might include experiences of the loss of employment, the death or disruption of a relationship, a traumatic accident, a move, or other personal loss. Out of such challenges arise the opportunity to change, to respond and grow, or to reject and run, refusing to accept the change because of the pain that accompanies it.

We are so familiar with the story of Abraham hearing God's call

to leave his country and become the father of God's people, that it
is strange to hear the story interpreted spiritually. A group of
spiritual Jews, living in Poland in the sixteenth century, called the
Hasidim, translated the story as meaning "Leave your country. Get
you out." They also heard in it this command: "Go into yourself.
Find out who you are, Abraham. Find out what your limits are.
Leave your family and your father's house, leave the training they
have given you. Leave behind your loyalty to them and go into the
land I will show you" (Genesis 12:1). "You see," God adds in an
offstage whisper, "you will not see it until you get in touch with
yourself. You will then see the land I am always showing you."

Jeremiah "Ate" God's Words

> *When your words came, I ate them;*
>   *they were my joy and my heart's delight.*
>   —Jeremiah 15:16

The truest meaning of words comes from the inside. Jesus "ate"
God's word. Jesus "enfleshed" God's word. Jesus was God's Word.
Edward Hays has written a story that expresses our need to "eat
God's word." It is called "The Board Meeting." It is an account of
a man who had been pronounced dead and then came back to life.
It might also have been a dramatic dream, but let the stranger tell
his story.

The Board Meeting[2]

I was traveling down a long, dark tunnel at the end of which I
found myself enveloped in a brilliant light, and as I came through
the cloud of light I saw in front of me a large, bright Tudor manor.
A doorman opened the door over which a brass plate read: "Private
Club, Members Only."

I entered a long paneled hallway at the end of which was a
bulletin board mounted on a stand. On it read a single announce-
ment: "Board of Directors Meeting Today." Beyond the sign was a
large, open common room. Everyone read, sat in silence, or spoke
softly with another member. There was a hushed reverence in the
room.

At the far end was a large brick fireplace with a circle of easy chairs around the blazing fire. Apparently it was the meeting place of the board of directors. Peals of laughter came from the circle, and since it was the only lively spot, I pulled up a chair and sat on the outside of the circle and stared at the identity of the members of the board. Directly across from me sat the Buddha. He was wearing a yellow straw hat, the kind made famous by W. C. Fields. The prophet Mohammed, to his right, wore a Mouseketeer cap with large black ears. To the left sat Moses in a tall, black top hat, and to his left sat Jesus, wearing a multicolored, medieval jester's cap with silver bells. Every time Jesus laughed, the bells would ring. Directly in front of me was the highest backed chair, but because of my position I could not see who was sitting there.

The four men were laughing, but no one else in the room seemed to notice. Mohammed, with a twinkle in his eye, teased Jesus about the bells. Moses pulled a rabbit from his top hat; Buddha told a joke, to which Jesus said, "Excellent, brother Buddha, but look at these people so proper, so trapped in ritual, stiff and formal." At that Jesus stood up and shouted, "Awake, the reign of God is at hand."

"Sit down, brother Jesus," said Mohammed. "Your words do not awaken anymore."

"Mohammed's right," agreed Moses. "Our words have become prisoners. Long ago people stopped telling the sacred stories and began to print them in books, which have become the prisons that hold our words."

"Yes," said Buddha sadly, "our words were once alive, but now they are frozen on pieces of paper."

"Sacred words should not be memorized but remembered," added Jesus. "When they are remembered they pass through the unique prism of each person. As they are retold they come alive with energy, enfleshed, and only words made flesh can challenge the human heart to greatness."

"Look at the bookshelves," said Buddha. "Beside the books that hold our words prisoner are commentaries, and next to them, commentaries on the commentaries, reflections by scholars, dissecting our words to make them more understandable—as though our words were too complex."

"And all these words are your words." Mohammed addressed the person who sat in front of me and had not yet spoken.

There was silence. Slowly, light began to surround the chair. Then out of the cloud a voice spoke—"I need someone to be a New Word to set my words free, to help them escape. Who will go this time?" When no one responded, the voice continued, "I need someone to show the people how to eat my words. Once my words are taken inside, made flesh and lived out, laughter will return. Who will go this time?"

"I have done my duty," said Moses. "Once is enough." Jesus, Buddha, and Mohammed all nodded their heads in agreement.

"You are right. Once is enough," the voice agreed.

A long empty pause followed, and then a strange thing happened. The great high-backed chair began to swivel around, and the intensity of the light became overpowering. Blinded by its brilliance, I covered my eyes, and out of that light came the voice, filled with affection and tenderness, "Will you, my beloved, will you go?"

We use the Bible, not as proof text, but as food, as nourishment for life in the spirit. God's word came to Jeremiah and there was joy, but not all of God's words to Jeremiah were joyous words. "Today I appoint you over nations and kingdoms to uproot and tear down, to destroy and overthrow, to build and to plant [Jer. 1:10, paraphrased]." God uproots in order that we may find our wings. God tears down so that we may learn how to build up for others. God destroys so that we put our faith in that which is permanent rather than in the temporal, visible things of the world. God builds up and plants, for words can feed. Words have the power to come alive in us and through us, to make us and our world more alive, more faithful.

The Gospel writers spend their coinage of words as misers. Words are very important. The word of the Lord has something unique to say to each of us. One more word to Jeremiah: "Before I formed you in the womb I knew you [Jer. 1:5]."

God knows each of us personally, and that is why God's word to us is personal, even directed to us before we are in the womb. "Before you were born, I set you apart," God says. "I am only a child," said Jeremiah. "Do not say I am only a child. You must go to everyone I send you to and say whatever I command you. Do not be afraid of them, for I am with you and will rescue you." Then the Lord reached out his hand and touched my mouth and said, "Now I put my words in your mouth [Jer. 1:5–9]." God feeds us with God's word and through that word asks each of us, "Will you, my beloved, will you go?"

Bread and Jesus' Temptations

Jesus said, "I am the bread of life." He is the Word made flesh to dwell among us, to feed us. Knowing the unity of the body and the spirit, he fed the people both physical and spiritual food. The tempter, too, knew the unity of body and spirit and the people's need for nourishment. After forty days without bread, the tempter came to Jesus, telling him to turn the stones into bread [Luke 4:1–14]. "If you are the Son of God, tell this stone to become bread." But Jesus answered, "It is written . . ." Praise God, we have the Word and the words, "for one does not live on bread alone." We seek bread, living bread, at the banquet, but only Spirit and scripture feed us with the food we need in order to survive.

The tempter persisted. He led Jesus up to a "high place" and showed him the kingdoms of the world, as he shows us. He shows us our ego desires and says, "Worship me," and (it is so subtle) we do. But Jesus answered, "The scripture says, 'Worship the Lord your God and serve God only [Luke 4:8, TEV]!'"

We are told to test the spirits. Whom are we serving—God, ourselves, the world, or the tempter? Still the tempter persisted. Now the third time with religious power, the temple. "Test God, and throw yourself down."

But Jesus replied, "You must not put the Lord your God to the test [TEV]." Do not test God through your prayers, be they for healing or for the poor or for the captive; but worship and trust God, for God's wisdom is not our wisdom.

But still one more time the tempter tries with us, "Well, good for you, you are growing in the Spirit," and this for us is the greatest temptation of all. Perhaps God in God's wisdom and love is even using the tempter to teach and strengthen us, to make us aware of how subtle and pervasive the temptations of the world are, to help us know how much we need each other and God.

Jesus gave us a hint when he said, "It is written." So thy words,

Lord, are not only a lamp unto my feet but a sword and shield in my hand.

There is a saying that no one who has not been tempted, who has not experienced the dark night and the deep hunger, can enter the kingdom of God. There is a Satan in each of us, whispering doubt as to our ability or, even more important, God's ability, spreading fear in all the dark places, counseling compromise by telling us we are too weak to make clear decisions or take serious risks, robbing us of hope and with it, health. It is then we need Jesus' words and Jesus' presence to heal our blindness, to open our ears, to teach us to see and hear and trust.

Biblical Praying

Your Light May Go Out

A student of Tendai, a philosophical school of Buddhism, came to the Zen abode of Gasan as a pupil. When he was departing a few years later, Gasan warned him: "Studying the truth speculatively is useful as a way of collecting preaching material. But remember that unless you meditate constantly your light of truth may go out."[3]

There are different breads at the banquet. There is a rich diversity in the foods and in the guests themselves. I used to be disturbed by the fact that Christians could not agree on using the same words in their prayer of unity, the prayer of Our Lord. I would pause after the words, "And forgive us our . . ." Recently, however, I caught the glory of the words *debts* and *trespasses* said at the same time. There was a unity in that diversity.

There is diversity in the way persons celebrate being with God or living life in the Spirit. Some pray ready-made prayers to keep in touch with "sound doctrine" or to remember the things they ought to ask. Some advocate spontaneous praying; others, meditation, contemplation, or silence. While some prefer praying aloud, others sit in solitude; still others pray for action and are summoned and sent. Some people pray with the words of scripture that Jesus used to refute Satan.

When Israel was in bondage to Egypt, she looked forward to her freedom, and God sent Moses to lead the people. When they came to the Red Sea, with the Egyptian army close behind with chariots and weapons, the sea blocked Israel's way to freedom. They knew they would drown if they entered the waters. At the edge they huddled on the shore, unable to retreat or to go forward. Pharaoh and his soldiers were coming closer each second, so that the Israelites could see the sun shining on their swords. They cried out to Moses, "What have you done to us?" And God said, "Tell the people to go forward on dry ground through the sea." Moses stretched out his hand over the sea to part the waters and told the people to go through, but they simply stared at him, for the waters had not yet parted. Could they trust God? Then in complete surrender to the Lord, they stepped into the sea as a strong east wind divided the waters and they crossed on dry land. They left the shore as slaves but came out on the other side free people.

Biblical praying is trust in God.

Using the Shema as a "Mantra"

Mantra is Sanskrit for a specific sound, a single word or group of words, a musical sound or chant, repeated as a means of focusing consciousness to assist in the work of meditation. Its purpose is to still our minds to become receptive to enter into the presence of God. (In the East various works of art also are used to aid meditation, such as icons in the Eastern Orthodox tradition.)

It is believed that the prayers, benedictions, and blessings of the mantras balance the curses of the world. For the Christian, the most familiar mantra is the Jesus Prayer of the Russian pilgrim from the Greek Orthodox Church. His story is told in *The Way of the Pilgrim*, an anonymous work written between 1855 and 1861 to introduce to the laity a way of expanding their awareness of God and their love for God through Christ. The pilgrim tells of hearing the words of Paul in church, "Pray without ceasing," but never any words about how to do this, so he searched and searched. At last he found an old man who gave him an answer: "Sit down alone and in silence. Lower your head, shut your eyes, breathe out gently, and imagine yourself looking into your own heart. Let your mind, or rather, your thoughts, flow from your head down to your heart and pray while breathing: 'Lord Jesus Christ have mercy'. Whisper the words gently, or say them in your mind. Discard all other thoughts. Be serene, persevere, and repeat them over and over." He was urged to say the prayer of the heart 3,000 times a day, then 6,000, and at last 12,000![4]

The people of the Old Testament believed that the name created the reality. God's name is the revelation of God's being. In the New Testament the name of Jesus presents a salvational experience: "Salvation is found in no one else, for there is no other name under heaven given by which we must be saved [Acts 4:12, paraphrased]."

The early Eastern Christians experienced the power of Jesus' name as a presence among them. It was not until the fourteenth century, however, that the Jesus Prayer, a prayer of surrendering to the Spirit, of dying to inordinate self-love and ultimately of achieving a way of life, became the words used to call upon Jesus' name, as he had exhorted his disciples: "My Father will give you whatever you ask in my name [John 16:23]."

Mohandas Gandhi once said that reciting God's name with faith would cure an individual of any disease. Among the Hindus such praying is called the Remembrance of the Name.

As a means of spiritual enlargement, mantras are either given by a spiritual guide or chosen by persons from their own spiritual awareness. They are thus rooted in the total context of the individual's life.

When Jesus was asked the question, "What must I do to be saved?" he replied, "You shall love the Lord your God and God only shall you serve." He spoke the words of the Shema,[5] Deuteronomy 6:4-5: "Hear, O Israel, the Lord our God, the Lord is one. Love the Lord your God with all your soul and with all your strength." Israel was a praying people, and Jesus was led and fed by scripture.

Last summer I participated in a class on Jewish mysticism led by Ted Falcon, a rabbi and psychologist well versed in transcendental meditation and scripture. He told about one day asking himself, "Is there nothing in my own heritage to enrich my life in the spirit?" Turning within he listened to the symbols and words that appeared, and he chose the Shema. For a year and a half he used the six phrases in his daily living. Then the following dramatic episode confirmed the process as vital, as the phrases remained in his consciousness meditationally when they were needed to connect him to the world. As he was driving through the mountains near Los Angeles, a heavy crane from a truck fell on his car, splitting it in two and pinning him inside. As he waited in agony, he unconsciously prayed the Shema, which he said "saved my life."

The Shema tells us to put these words on our hearts (where we feel) and in our minds (where we think), to recite them morning and evening, when we sit in our houses or go on our way, to let them be in our consciousness always: "Pray without ceasing."

"Hear." Listen. The mystics taught the importance of silence. "Pay attention!" the Shema says. Slow down. Hear the "still small voice." Taste the silence within.

"O Israel." Jacob, terrified over meeting his brother whom he had cheated, sent his wife on ahead and prepared himself. His surprise was to meet the one—angel, man, or God—with whom he wrestled all night in order to receive a new name, a "blessing." He left wounded from his struggle, but he did not run away. He may have limped, but he was blessed. "Your name is no more Jacob but Israel because you have contended with God . . . and have prevailed [Gen. 32:28, paraphrased]."

"The Lord, our God." The heart of Jewish mysticism is the name of God. "He Is," "What Is," "Eternal God," the Tetragrammaton (a word of four letters; see Exodus 3:13–15 and accompanying notes) is the secret name of God, not to be pronounced, for we cannot contain "What Is" in a word. Being is the root of our being, and there is in each of us the "holy of holies" in which we can come alive to life in the Spirit.

"Is One." The Lord is the Place where everything is. The Eternal One who is many, the transcendent God, is God's oneness, wholeness, God's Being Itself, which is too big to be spoken. Yet we believe that God's Spirit, the Holy Spirit, is present within us. God calls us to our uniqueness, our blessing, the destiny God has in store for us that is too good to be true. It is a paradox that while we keep our own uniqueness and God keeps God's, each human being is an aspect of the whole. Each of us carries a piece of creation.

"And you shall love the Lord your God with all your heart, and with all your soul, and with all your might [Deut. 6:5]." The consequence of hearing and praying the Shema is love. It is how we think, feel, and act in the world. Real love is honoring oneself and the other in the being of God, who is Love. Praying the Shema awakens a deep appreciation for all.

The Psalms: A Book of Prayers

The psalms were bread for the Desert Fathers and Mothers in the wilderness. They ate their bread at the banquet and were fed by the word of God. Those whose vocation is in the church also live on the psalms. The Benedictine and Cistercian monks chant their way through the Psalter once a week, reciting the psalms after meals and during the Mass. They interrupt their work to sing psalms during the day hours and their sleep to chant them in the middle of the night.

The psalms are passionate pleas for mercy and help, as well as expressions of joy and praise. They were written as honest and spontaneous self-expressions of desperation and complaint, unpremeditated cries for help: "How long, O Lord? Will you forget me forever? How long will you hide your face from me [Ps. 13:1]?"

Out of the dark night of the soul the psalmist cries in confusion and panic, and when the passion is poured out in words, suddenly the mood changes and resolution takes place within, a transformation. Where doubt and despair reigned, hope now takes its place. Inner resources are integrated, if even for a moment.

The psalms are religious poetry, fingers pointing to God. They are bridges to God, which, when we have crossed them, are no longer needed. They are the garment or the flesh for what had been before invisible and inaudible. These are a few of the many metaphors for the psalms, for understanding the unique way God is present to us when we interiorize their words. This interiorization integrates our faith, our feeling, and our experience. Praying the psalms connects us with the roots of our faith tradition and with praying Christians around the world.

Jesus As a Teacher of Prayer

"And Jesus went out to pray." All the rest is commentary.

Jesus took time for prayer that nurtured and taught, forgave and healed. His spiritual guide was God. Is it possible that when he was in the hills alone with God Jesus was weak? When we come to God we can be weak and fearful, letting go of our burdens and concerns to be comforted as well as challenged and corrected. Jesus took time alone with God in order to know God's love, protection, mercy, and guidance. We do not have a record of what he said when he went into the hills to pray, but we know that scripture ministered and fed him, for he knew God's word "by heart."

The disciples came to Jesus and said, "Teach us to pray." They did not say "how to pray" but "to pray." And Jesus told them a story: "Suppose one of you has a friend, and he goes to him at midnight and says, 'Friend, lend me three loaves of bread' . . ." Jesus goes on to say that although the one inside does not want to be bothered, "because of the man's persistence he will get up and give him as much as he needs."

"So I say to you: Ask and it will be given to you; seek and you will find; knock and the door will be opened to you [Luke 11:5–13]."

He also told them a story about two people at prayer. The story of the publican and the Pharisee shows two contrasting ways of praying (Luke 18:9–14). Prayer lives in humility and in persistence, for Jesus also told the story of the widow who kept coming to the judge with the plea, "Grant me justice against my adversary." He refused. She persisted. He continued to refuse. Then, because she bothered him, he granted her wish. If the unjust judge will do that, Jesus pointed out, "Will not God bring about justice for God's chosen ones, who cry out day and night [Luke 18:1–8]?" Jesus encouraged disciplined seekers. He told his hearers to pray in private, in their "closets" (Matthew 6:6, paraphrased), and when he raised Lazarus from the dead, he first prayed (John 11:41–42). When the disciples tried to cast out evil spirits and failed, Jesus told them, "This kind can come out only by prayer [Mark 9:29, paraphrased]."

Jesus prayed alone on the hills (Luke 6:12), very early in the morning (Mark 1:35), in the congregation, in crises, before decisions, and as prophet, priest, and king. He prayed intercessory prayers: "I have prayed for you, that your faith may not fail [Luke 22:32]." And mothers brought children for him to touch and pray for (Matthew 19:13). He told the people to "pray for them who despitefully use you and persecute you [Matt. 5:44, paraphrased]."

Prayer is love in exercise, and in his agony in the garden, Jesus' deepest, most heartfelt prayer was, "Thy will be done [Luke 22:42, paraphrased]." "Heartfelt" was the way Jesus prayed.

An old monk said: "When I was your age, I was wondering

where would be the best place to pray. So I asked Jesus, and he said, 'Why don't you go into the heart of my Father.' So I did. I went into the heart of the Father, and all these years that is where I have prayed. Now I believe."6

Jesus teaches that to believe is to place our mind in our heart, to use our imagination, where we encounter God. To believe is to sing and dance our creeds rather than debate them.

Spirit in the Bible

Reading the Bible is exciting because God's *ruach* blows through the words and we know not from where it comes nor to where it is going. In Hebrew *ruach* means God's breath, the Spirit of God. This mysterious gift of the Spirit sent by God to make all things new transforms us and the created world. Disembodied, abstract theology requires the breath of the Spirit, for to explain rationally, to make affirmations of faith understandable, to use words to control what gives life in God's name—this rational attitude cannot stand up against the Spirit conveyed to us in the words of scripture. Scriptural words invite the imagination to sing, the heart to pound, the truth to transform and deliver. They feed our spirit.

God fed the Hebrews with manna in their wanderings in the wilderness. Jesus fed the hungry people (John 6:1–15) with bread and fish, and God feeds us today through the word, the word that says, "And the Spirit of God was moving over the face of the waters [Gen. 1:2]." The tellers and writers of the story of God saw the Spirit of God as the agent of creation, the divine principle at work in the world, the source of physical, spiritual, and moral life.

In the Genesis garden story (2:7) God breathed into the nostrils of the first creature "the breath of life; and the human became a living being." When we receive the Spirit of God, we become living souls, totalities of body and spirit. The word *ruach* is the same word that is used for wind. Where God works, the air is stirred and life is felt. God's breath is the principle of life, creative energy, vitality. To be "inspired" is to be given power beyond our own. God's "inspiring breath" grants life in creation, and in re-creation, new life.

Ezekiel 37:1–14 contains Ezekiel's vision of the valley of dry bones, which symbolize the Israelites in exile in Babylon. The story of the dry bones is helpful for understanding the doctrine of the Spirit. The Lord God said to Ezekiel: speak to the dry bones, "Behold, I will cause breath to enter you, and you shall live [37:5]." "A new heart I will give you, and a new spirit I will put within you; and I will take out of your flesh the heart of stone and give you a heart of flesh. And I will put my spirit within you [36:26]." God is breathing back into Israel a new spirit, just as the wind entered the dead bodies to give them life. Ezekiel obeyed his vision, his inner voice, and spoke for the Lord. That very prophesying of the return in some sense effected the return. The "word" accomplished that for which it was sent.

John wrote of the Word as Jesus, the Christ, by whose words we are fed. Luke wrote that through Jesus, the Lord has "filled the hungry with good things [1:53]." And much of Jesus' "feeding" was done when he answered questions, such as "What must I do to inherit eternal life?"; "Who is my neighbor?"; "How can I be born again?"; "Are you the one we seek?"; "Why do your disciples not fast?"; "Who is my mother, and who are my brothers?"; "Who do people say that the Son of man is?"; "Who is greatest in the kingdom of heaven?"; and "Lord, how often shall my brother or sister sin against me, and I forgive?"

As we stumble over the furniture of life, we bring our own questions to Jesus. Although scripture can lead us into an encounter with God, it can never substitute for that encounter. As Ezekiel wrote of the Spirit's giving rebirth, new life, so too did John, in the dialogue between Jesus and Nicodemus (John 3:1–15). Nicodemus came to Jesus at night, in the dark, with a question, the question of the meaning of existence. He came to Jesus for an answer, since Jesus was "a teacher come from God." Nicodemus was a Pharisee and member of the Sanhedrin. He had plenty of answers. As a faithful Jew he had *the* answer: the Law. He stands for a community that has knowledge of scripture, for the persons in John's Gospel are both historical and symbolic. Nicodemus represented official Judaism before the claims of Christ. And Jesus' reply, "Truly, truly, I say to you, unless one is born anew, one cannot see the kingdom of God," became the basic text for the dialogue between Jesus and Nicodemus.

John drew on the known traditional sayings of Jesus, writing his Gospel in the dialogue style, a popular kind of writing at that time. Even though this form of dialogue, which in John becomes discourse (question, answer, incomprehension or misunderstanding, restatement), was popular at the time, we can imagine that Nicodemus would have been legitimately confused. Jesus seemed to give an answer for which there was no question, and Nicodemus was a materialist. Poor Nicodemus! His thinking blocked his awareness. From his perception Jesus' answer was preposterous, and he said so: "How can one be born when one is old? Can we enter a second time into our mothers' wombs and be born?"

Salvation, health, the soul's health all speak of a need for transcendent reality, for spiritual food, and for new life in the Spirit today. Religion can be either the way to a spiritual life or a substitute for it. When religion teaches only about God without providing "rebirth"—education into being open to the Spirit and an environment in which to experience the presence of God—it runs the risk of caring for only the intellect and ignoring the spiritual, inner person. Creeds, dogma, ritual, cannot replace experience and faith. They will inform and enrich and provide the vehicles for experiential knowing, but they can never be substitutes for a living relationship with God. Spirituality arises when there is renewal in the church, for it is the church's source of life and its nourishment. Just as men and women dry up without food and drink, so they become hollow without an awareness of God's presence in their lives.

Nicodemus would have already been acquainted with the Spirit from his own tradition (see Genesis and Ezekiel above). His question simply furthered the dialogue and called forth Jesus' restatement. Jesus adds that one must be born "of water and the Spirit," "born anew," begotten from above, from God. How does this occur? "The wind blows where it wills." Jesus uses both meanings of the word *ruach*, God's breath and wind. He uses the unpredictability of the nature of wind to represent the spontaneous activity of God, Spirit in renewal. Still Nicodemus does not understand Jesus, for he says, "How can this be?" Jesus replies, "If I have told you earthly things and you do not believe, how can you believe if I tell you heavenly things?" This kingdom into which one comes through spiritual rebirth is only revealed by the one sent by God.

Jesus' answer was the faith community's response to Jesus' death and resurrection: "We know, have encountered, the one in whom we believe." Jesus did not answer Nicodemus with a rational interpretation. Nor does he us, but with his living presence. John 3 keeps the dialogue going. The questioning, listening, affirming, challenging, probing are what happens through scripture and God's feeding. Nicodemus fades out of the story, and we do not know his response in words, though we know of his actions later. Did he return to his book of prayers, the psalms, and cry out: "Create in me a clean heart, O God, and put a new and right spirit within me. Cast me not away from thy presence, and take not thy holy Spirit from me [Ps. 51:10–11]"? With the psalmist, and perhaps Nicodemus, we too pray for life in the spirit:

Make me new, other than I am. Give me your Spirit. Not a new face, not a new piece of clothing, not a new job nor wife or husband or parents or children, but a new beginning, a new birth begotten from above, a new me from inside out—a loving heart, a renewed spirit, a reconciling tongue—and turn me toward the light, your Light, to make me new and other than I am.

In Paul's eighth chapter to the Romans the Spirit is referred to no fewer than twenty times. The Spirit here means both the Spirit of God—the breath of life, the energizing, creative principle of life—and the Spirit of Jesus—the seal of the resurrection, the sign of the new age and the new being in Christ. Other metaphors for the Holy Spirit are the Counselor, the Comforter, and "God's love poured into our hearts [Rom. 5:5]." It is the Spirit who "helps us in our weakness; for we do not know how to pray as we ought, but the Spirit intercedes for us with sighs too deep for words [8:26]." "For you did not receive the spirit of slavery to fall back into fear, but you have received the spirit of adoption as children of God [8:15]." Through the Spirit you and I are heirs, God's adopted and natural children. "For all who are led by the Spirit of God are [heirs] of God [8:14]."

Paul lifted up this life in the Spirit, which gives us our freedom and our inheritance, not slavery but sonship, not despair but "daughtership," not fear but faith. So we too cry with Jesus, "Abba! Father!" God is Spirit, seeking us through Christ, reaching us in the Spirit.

It is the Holy Spirit who births our faith and provides the power of God's grace to keep our faith and love alive, abundantly alive and alert. This faith works to supply the head (contemplative thought) and the heart (active love), for love without intelligence is an empty emotion, and intelligence without love is empty knowledge. The Holy Spirit relates the remembered word (the Christian story) to the present situation and thus renews its power. To live "in the Spirit" is to exercise this power, this energy, the energy of faith that stirs up action to perform the deeds of love and peace in the world. Through the Spirit, God feeds and renews us. For God is in a South African prison today, as well as in a Roman one yesterday; in the speech of a wandering evangelist today, as in an Ezekiel of yesterday; in the warnings of the ecologist as in a Jeremiah; in the death of one small, unknown child as in the deaths of Steve Biko, Martin Luther King Jr., Dietrich Bonhoeffer, Joan of Arc, Stephen, and John of Patmos. The Spirit of God can be in the word of your wife or husband, of your child or parent, of you or me; for God is alive and active and still working through the Holy Spirit today as in the past.

We consider the words of the prophet:

> And it shall come to pass afterward,
>   that I will pour out my spirit on all flesh.
>   —Joel 2:28

To understand the Holy Spirit is not easy. Walter Wangerin, Jr., a contemporary preacher, tells of being told as a youngster, "Wally, you are the *spittin'* image of your grandpa." The remark led him to wonder whether he had to chew tobacco as his grandpa had chewed. Twenty-seven years later, however, he learned the meaning of the words when one of his parishioners spoke of her husband who had recently been buried. She remarked of her son: "Arthur Junior is the spittin' image of his daddy." Wangerin lunged at the poor woman, asking her to repeat what she had said. Then he queried, "You mean like spit? spittle?" he asked. She repeated her words: "Spee-it." She was saying "spirit."[7] It can take many years to know how to live in communion with God's Spirit. Yet, to do so is our birthright as Christians.

Chapter 3

Religious Experience

Varieties of Religious Experience

Religious experience is the total experience of a religious person. Each of us is unique, blessed with different gifts, as Paul wrote: "Now there are varieties of gifts, but the same Spirit [1 Cor. 12:4]." God feeds us with a variety of breads, for temperaments and tastes vary. Some are fed through prayer and meditation, some by scripture or sacred story, others through dream or ritual, nature or music, service or love. The divine meets and feeds us at the point of our personal concerns.

Without a variety of consciousnesses the total human understanding and experience of the Divine would suffer. Even praying varies, from the earliest Christian mystics (some advocated violence and daily mortification of the body), to those who sing and dance and cry with joy or sadness, to those who work for justice and freedom, who integrate the courage of the prophet with the joy of the mystic. Martin Luther said that our prayers should be frequent and short, yet he spent hours in prayer. The twentieth-century Jewish theologian and mystic Martin Buber said that all prayer is summoning and sending. Others state that it is the work of love, more effective than anything else in increasing our love for God. Whatever our definition of prayer or whatever our religious experience, it reveals our worldview.

Not only are we each different, but life changes constantly. George Bernard Shaw once said that the only person who behaved sensibly was his tailor, who took his measure anew each time he saw him, while others went on with their old "measurements" and expected him to fit them. And William James observed that "just as there is no one religious emotion [fear, love, awe, joy, etc.], so also there would seem to be no one specific and essential kind of religious object and no one specific and essential kind of religious activity."[1]

Each of us experiences the presence and work of God in his or her own way. "But," you say, "I have never had such an experience." Yet most of us have. One purpose of this book is to help us value times when we have felt God's presence and to help us prepare to do so again. Religious experience cannot be proved. In stuttering words it may be described. No matter what the other thinks about it, the one who has it possesses the great treasure, the pearl of great price that provides meaning and beauty and gives a new splendor to the world. It is through our human experience that we meet God.

Faith Imagination: Visions and Voices

Religious experience is closely associated with imagination, intuition, and wonder. It is not that God is absent if we do not have these attributes, but that through them we are aware of God. Yet God is here, whether or not we recognize God. Locating the consciousness of an experience in the imagination does not invalidate its reality. This openness to God's presence is spirituality.

Spirituality uses the imagination as a way of encountering God in Christ now. Through the imagination God can feed, guide, strengthen, and heal us. Living life in the Spirit is to live a life of imagination, where one's perception and posture of wholeness is in relation to God and to the world. For me, imagination is seeing from the inside. Let us recall that many a blind person experiences the world of images having never even seen from the outside.

Imagination based on faith is a way of seeing without eyes. Western, rationalistic materialism, however, does not understand such seeing. It teaches us to accept only what we can experience with the senses, and it is, therefore, unaware of the power and possibilities we have within. Paul wrote of "the power at work within us to do far more abundantly than all we ask or think [Eph. 3:20]."

Imagination can awaken the inner world, and love can transform images into presences. Such seeing is not acquired by analytical thought but by waiting. Gerard Manley Hopkins, the great Roman Catholic poet, called such vision "inscape," the ability to see God's creation with an inner, as well as an outer, vision. Some call this "imagination blessed by God."

The world partly comes to be how it is imagined. It was late when Gregory Bateson, the famous anthropologist, came to this idea. Writing his last book while dying, his daughter asked him, why he now chose to write. "For me," Bateson replied, "after fifty years of pushing these ideas about [religion], it has slowly become clear that muddleheadedness is not necessary. I have always hated muddleheadedness and always thought it was a necessary condition for religion. But it seems that that is not so. You see, they preach faith, and they preach surrender. But I wanted clarity."[2]

To awaken to the wonder of a world greater than the one we see and touch is the function of the imagination. The rich young ruler, who came to Jesus because he wanted to enter life fully, went away with a heavy heart because he lacked imagination. He had great material wealth and was poor in seeing what mattered.

In order to balance the physical and the spiritual, that is, to move toward wholeness, we need faith. Maintaining and acquiring wholeness consists of adopting the point of view of faith, of trust beyond belief. In this we are fed and developed by our faith imagination, supported by the sacred biblical story. The theologian William Lynch calls faith "the superb life of the imagination," and Amos Wilder said that just because we lack imagination is no reason to think that the ancients did also. We are body and spirit: whole. There is physical and spiritual reality: one. In our need for integration of the body and spirit, we have turned once again to recognize the power of the imagination to refresh, strengthen, guide, and heal. A world without imagination is unable to cope with immaterial, unseen spiritual reality.

The cultivation of the imagination makes us human and sensitive. It holds the key to coming to terms with one's own story. Through imagination, stories—our own and others'—reveal Reality. Stories provide a landscape of opportunities for emotional response: to feel, to weep, to laugh, to love, even to enter the emotions of others, seeing through their eyes and stepping into their skins to share their problems, quests, and adventures. Jesus used his imagination. He referred to himself as bread, living water, truth, blood, light, a door, a vine, a road, the word, a shepherd, and a lamb. He walked on water, turned water into wine, sent demons into swine, and calmed the waves. Nature was responsive to him. Neither Jesus nor the biblical writers were literalists. They used their imaginations to see and to tell.

With the unsuspected and untapped source of power for life in the imagination, we too can use all our faculties to reach the core of our humanity. One way to do so is through "fantasy" prayer. Anthony de Mello, one of the world's foremost spiritual guides, wrote a book of spiritual exercises in which seventeen of the forty-seven are placed under the heading "fantasy."[3] Far from serving as an escape from reality, these exercises encourage withdrawal into silence and the imagination. They help persons perceive reality and plunge more deeply into it with energy and confidence. From the wealth of his experience de Mello wrote that, when retreatants said they could not pray with their imaginations, he used to tell them to pray as they could. But he became certain that with a little practice everyone can acquire untold emotional and spiritual riches by developing the power to fantasize.

The perception of the divine is an intuition that is not attained directly by any process of reasoning. It is the gift of the Spirit, faith. It is the capacity for vision. "I will pour out my Spirit on all people; your sons and daughters will prophesy, your old men will dream dreams, your young men will see *visions* [Joel 2:8 and Acts 2:17, emphasis added]." The Bible asks us to extend our imaginations into unknown territories: burning bushes that are not consumed, men in fiery furnaces, persons wrestling with angels, blind eyes opened, deaf ears unstopped, and the lame leaping as the hart eager for water. If we cannot imagine, how will we recognize Christ among us?

The Bible records many visions. God's covenant with Abram occurred in a vision. As the sun was setting, Abram fell into a deep sleep, and a thick and dreadful darkness came over him. Then the Lord said to him, "Know of a surety that your descendants will be sojourners in a land that is not theirs [Gen. 15:12–13]." The familiar story of Cornelius' vision is recorded in Acts 10:3. One day at about three in the afternoon Cornelius distinctly saw an angel of God. Peter's vision is recorded in Acts 10:9–19.

Afterwards, "While Peter was pondering the vision, the Spirit said to him . . ." And "During the night Paul had a vision of a man of Macedonia standing and begging him, 'Come over to Macedonia and help us [Acts 16:9, paraphrased]'." The entire book of Revelation is given to John by an angel in a vision: "The horses and riders I saw in my vision. . . [Rev. 9:17]."

The psalmists wrote with imagination. In Psalm 18:10 we read: "God mounted the cherubim and flew; God soared on the wings of the wind." Paul wrote of his own experience: "I must boast; there is nothing to be gained by it, but I will go on to visions and revelations of the Lord. I know a man in Christ who fourteen years ago was caught up to the third heaven—whether in the body or out of the body I do not know, God knows [2 Cor. 12:1–2]."

Some are suspect of such visions and voices, and even the great mystics warned against accepting visions and voices at their face value as messages from God. Yet without believing we eliminate possibility from the beginning. Evelyn Underhill in her masterful study *Mysticism* asks whether the voices or visions are the pictures of desires, or morbid hallucinations, or "the violent effort of the self to translate something impressed upon its deeper being, some message received from without, which projects this sharp image and places it before the conscious?"[4] Her chapter "Vision and Voices" further answers this question. Voices and visions convey wisdom, assurance, and confidence to the simple and the wise and to those tormented by doubt. Voices and visions feed the spirit with courage and creative energy, strength and direction, leaving both the body and the spirit stronger than before. There are also times when the visions are tormenting and terrible. We are told to "test the spirits," to discern which are good and which are evil, and we do well to do so.

Gratitude for clarifying voices and visions has led to their being called "sweet surprises." I once had a dream when I was deeply agitated over a decision. I awoke hearing the words, "You will know what to do when you get there." The words have provided assurance through the years.

Mystics, however, are distressed over the impossibility of describing what they experience. Angela of Foligno wrote: "At times God comes into the soul without being called; and He instills into her fire, love, and sometimes sweetness; . . . but a certain doubt

remains; for the soul has not the certitude that God is in her. . . .
And beyond this the soul receives the gift of seeing God. . . . This
beholding, whereby the soul can behold no other thing, is so
profound that it grieves me that I can say nothing of it. It is not a
thing which can be touched or imagined, for it is ineffable."[5]
Julian of Norwich received her "showings," or revelations, and
then had her doubts. She asked questions and finally accepted
their authority. For twenty years afterwards she prayerfully reflected
upon them and in that way received instruction.

The imagination must be used or it will be "taken away," which
reminds us of Jesus' words: "Those who have will get more until
they grow rich, while those who have not will lose even the little
they have" and "Though seeing, they do not see; though hearing,
they do not hear or understand. . . . But blessed are your eyes
because they see, and your ears because they hear [Matt. 13:10–13,
paraphrased]."

How then do we begin? Once, while I was suffering from a
traumatic event in which I felt that all my inner resources had
dried up, a counselor told me to accept my feelings and use my
imagination. She advised that I simply sit still to experience the
emotion I was feeling. If possible I was to name it and talk with it,
asking questions concerning its origin, "Where did you come
from?" and its purpose, "What is the meaning of this? What are
you trying to tell me?" Sitting in silence, waiting open and
receptive to images, visions, or voices, while inviting Jesus' presence within, is a way to begin to experience the value of the
imagination.

Charles Williams in *The Greater Trumps* (the story of the dance
of the Tarot cards and their messages and of the importance of "the
fool," whom no one but the cards can explain) wrote of Nancy:
"That Christmas there came into Nancy's life with the mystery of
the Tarots a new sense of delighted amazement," for now she saw
all the world differently: holy and beautiful. Nothing was certain,
but everything was safe—that was part of the mystery of Love.
"Nothing mattered beyond the full moment in which she could
live to her utmost in the power and according to the laws of the
dance."[6]

The imagination invites us to live with Love. And Richard
Vieth closed his *Holy Power, Human Pain* by writing of the

Salvadoran refugees' celebrating Christmas out of nothing and seeing themselves as stronger than all the powers arrayed against them. "In the weird logic of my imagination, I see them as an incarnation of Jesus' words: 'In the world you have tribulation; but be of good cheer, I have overcome the world (John 15:33).' "[7] It is in the "weird logic" of *imagination* that we are fed at the banquet.

Dreams

The weird logic of imagination sometimes provides religious experiences of sublime harmony, of the numinous, of the spirit that blows where and when it will through the dream. Such an experience is a source of strength and confidence, the foundation for all future faith. It can be the turning point in a person's psychological development. Paul would call it conversion.

Dreams have the potential to awaken us, warn us, and guide us to wholeness and healing. Some people dream images, and others dream words. I remember waking from a dream to hear the words, "Awake, to sleep!" It was fun pondering whether the words meant, "Wake up to what dreams can mean" or "Sleep, in order to awaken." To me they were the same: awake to find the voice, the direction within; be open to the power and revelation of dream. The dream spoke to me of the need for bringing to consciousness the unconscious and for balancing "awareness" with the unconscious, the intuition. The unconscious functions to complement the conscious mind. The unconscious contains a psychic energy that pushes toward expression and integration with conscious life. To dream is to sleep, to let go of conscious thinking and will and "drop down into" the unconscious, a metaphor for sensing a different reality from daytime awareness.

The word *dream* has two denotations: the conscious wish or hope that motivates our actions; and the unconscious visualizations that give us energy, information, and intuitive insights. In the unconscious are the creative forces of the imagination that reconcile our outward life with our inner life to give us meaning and purpose. The whole of reality cannot be contained or experienced in the waking hours alone. That which we experience during sleep we call dreaming, an unconscious state. Visions are the conscious dreams we imagine when we awake. The biblical writers understood dreams and visions as revelatory of God, as ways in which God spoke to men and women.

When Miriam and Aaron rebuked Moses because of his Cushite wife, they asked, "Has the LORD spoken only through Moses? Hasn't he also spoken through us?"

"Then the LORD came down in a pillar of cloud; he stood at the entrance to the Tent and summoned Aaron and Miriam. When both of them stepped forward, he said, 'Listen to my words: When a prophet of the LORD is among you, I reveal myself to that one in visions, I speak in dreams [Num. 12:5–6, paraphrased].'"

Thus, God is established as the source of visions and dreams. In this respect, the entire Bible is the story of God's revelations through the conscious and unconscious expression of the religious experiences of the biblical prophets and writers.

At Gibeon the Lord appeared to Solomon during the night in a dream (1 Kings 3:5, 15). The priest Zechariah, chosen by lot to go into the temple of the Lord to burn incense, saw an angel of the Lord (Gabriel), who told him his wife Elizabeth would bear a child (Luke 1:5–23). The appearance of an angel is equated with a dream or vision (v. 22). God sent the angel to Mary (Luke 1:26), and to Joseph an angel of the Lord appeared many times in a dream (Matthew 1:19–20; 2:13; 2:19–20; and 2:22). To the shepherds an angel of the Lord appeared (Luke 2:8–10).

God came to Abimelech in a dream (Genesis 20:3). Joseph and others had dreams (37:5; 40:8) and Joseph interpreted dreams (41:1, 16, 25). And "God spoke to Israel in a vision at night and called, 'Jacob! Jacob! [46:2, TEV]'." Ezekiel saw visions of God (Ezekiel 1:1), and the Spirit lifted him up (2:1–2; 3:12); the boy Samuel heard God's voice (1 Samuel 3:1–18). The entire book of Obadiah is a vision, beginning, "The vision of Obadiah," as is the "book of the vision of Nahum the Elkoshite"; and in the book of Job (Job 4:12–17) Eliphaz had a dream. Job complained that when he went to bed to be comforted with sleep, "even then you frighten me with dreams and terrify me with visions [7:14]."

The early church fathers believed until the emergence of Scholasticism and the Enlightenment that dreams were a means of revelation. They believed that dreams gave access to the same place of reality one could penetrate in meditation. John Sanford, Episcopal priest and practicing Jungian analyst, calls dreams "the forgotten language of God," insisting that dreams are facts and, in existing as such, have a function.

A dream is a mirror of personal meaning. It is the way we "story" our lives in sleep. Today many modern psychoanalysts speak of dreams as a voice of inner truth. Frances Wickes in *The Inner World of Choice* describes the dream of a five-year-old: "I dreamed that the world outside is all waves. Angels told me to die of my own accord. But God said, 'Don't do that.' If you die of your own accord when angels tell you, you step out on the waves and don't get anywhere. But if you die when God tells you, he takes you and cleans away all your ghosts, and you can walk on the water and come back and live all over again."[8]

The choice between life and death is ever recurrent. "Angels" represent innocence, the acceptance of a wish-fulfilling dream world. At least in this dream angels seem to point to the temptation to allow things to happen without choice, to be a spectator rather than a responsible participant. A rabbi said: "Angel! It is no great trick to be innocent up there. You don't have to choose, to raise children, to make money. Just you come down to earth and choose, raise children, and make money, and see if you can be an angel here!" If we listen to angels, as Wickes's child recounted, we do not "get anywhere," for consciousness stands above innocence. And when we lose our innocence we are no longer helpless. It is not only five-year-olds, however, who listen to "angel voices" and live their lives dreaming instead of living their dreams. The dream message was "reflect on your experience, discover meaning in your mistakes, listen to God, and then come back and live all over again." And Christ said that unless a person was born again of the Spirit he or she would not enter the kingdom of heaven. It is being born again that matters most.

Dreams can be invitations to come back and live all over again, to choose between life and death, to live our own thoughts and feelings, to fashion our own dreams into reality. They can serve as invitations to listen to God. "God takes you and cleans away all your ghosts," the child said. Ghosts represent the past, past memories of people, pains, rejections, unfulfilled dreams, paths not taken, choices not freely made. Becoming acquainted with ghosts robs them of their power to haunt. Naming ghosts can transform them into messengers.

Frances Wickes recounted another dream, as well, the dream of a man of fifty: "I dreamed that I have died in my sleep, but now I must be reawakened to die while I am awake and conscious." The man was a scientist. He lived freely in his chosen world, had married, fathered a family, and achieved success in his scientific life. But he had separated himself from his feelings and used them to keep others from intruding upon his busy life. When he had his dream, he was feeling failed by his family, and his irritation with them spilled over into an irritation with life. "The sterile finger of ego achievement had touched him with a sense of futility." The dream haunted him. He had died in his sleep. He was unconscious of feelings. At this time he had another dream, a dream of his father who was dead. That which lived long ago in our conscious life and is dead can be reborn in ghost or spirit form, ghosts that haunt or spirits that quicken. They live in our unconscious. From there the dreamer's father had ruled, forbidding feeling or irrational experience. Wickes wrote: "This voice of absolutism must die if the ghost is to be cleaned away by God and the spark of creative energy be reborn within him, lighting again the fires of emotion and original desire."

In his dream the man also saw a dead Christmas tree, a rootless, ghost tree with a green bird in its dead branches. The living Christmas tree of his childhood, a symbol of the divine child, had become a rootless thing of creed and dogma; his old beliefs had died. Yet in the dead tree's branches was the green bird of intuitive perception, a symbol of transformation, for a dead creed may contain a living symbol to quicken new life, a rebirth in the spirit. As the dreamer reached out his left hand to choose the dream, the bird flew to his wrist. "The green bird, the living spirit of the Christ tree, now goes with him when he leaves the place where the old life has died." His creative imagination took on new life, his perception of spiritual mystery returned, and the green bird became white, the symbol for the dove which descended on Jesus at his baptism with the words "This is my beloved son."

The dreamer came to the reality that he must die in order to be born into the new life of sonship, in order to enter the kingdom of wholeness and unity with God, to be one in the Spirit, to come back and live all over again "in newness because ego and Self have become reconciled through the death that is rebirth. . . . God must be rediscovered through personal experience, through consciousness" so that the dreamer may live his dream rather than dreaming his life.[9]

Both men and women from time to time need to let go of the angel voices, but it is women, discouraged to do so by prevailing social norms, who especially need to find their own voice so that they can freely choose to hear God's voice. The dreams of life and death are with us always, but they can awaken us to the reality of both.

Dreams come from the imagination and indicate where the dreamer's attention is. Sleep invites us to rest the conscious, working, rational mind. When the conscious mind lets go, normal rules do not apply. Space and time no longer follow logic but expand and contract. People from the past, dead and alive, mingle with the present; impossible possibilities are acted out; and mysterious solutions to problems are suggested. Dreams are irrational because they come from the unconscious. Nor are all dreams of pleasant places and people. Some of them mean heavy work, leaving the dreamer exhausted. Some dreams reveal parts of ourselves we do not wish to see. The conscious and unconscious struggle together; the angels war with the demons in our dreams. When angels appear in the New Testament, their first words are "Do not be afraid."

Recently, I had two dreams. In one I was driving a car that became stuck in the mud. I could not move the car no matter how hard I tried. There were others who tried to help me push the car out of the mud. Finally, I chose to walk away. The other dream was again of an automobile that had abandoned me. I was thrown from the car and left hanging precariously on a cliff over a deep abyss. I could feel the ground of the cliff crumbling beneath my fingers and hear the proverbial words echo in my ears, "Let go! Let go!" Two dreams of being stuck were, to my interpretation—for only the dreamer can interpret the dream—an invitation to become aware, responsible, and active. Dreams carry messages of meaning, but that meaning must be interpreted by its receiver. Though the dream is the seed, the potential, the work of actualizing the dream is done consciously. The individual awake must make a living connection with the dream, or it will remain an abstraction.

Today we are again approaching dreams as important manifestations of guidance and wisdom. In interpreting our dreams we can learn to cope with unrealistic fears and inhibitions, confront and conquer danger, work on and solve problems, gain a sense of freedom and power, and enjoy memories of people and places, music and books.

The Talmud says that dreams not interpreted are like letters not opened. The dream is its own best explanation. Though the interpretation of the dream is sometimes less subtle, rich, or affective than the dream itself, the dreamer must always become engaged as interpreter. It is the dreamer's emotional explanation of why the image was of this person rather than that, water instead of fire, and so on, that integrates the meaning and power of the dream. The personal details of the dream I mentioned earlier, the images of which were lost as I was awaking, may have faded but the words did not: "You will know what to do when you get there." Over and over these words have come into my consciousness since that dream, assuring me that I will know what to do when the time comes and eliminating unnecessary energy on worry over future, unknown events.

Ira Progoff describes the dreams of several of his patients in *The Symbolic and the Real.* My favorite story is of Mr. Hart, a fifty-year-old man who worked on his dream in a group of other "dream-workers." In the dream he found himself in front of a locked door. He had no key. He shoved, pushed, pried, used whatever force he had, but he could not open the door. All he accomplished was to bruise himself. In the dream he felt physical pain as well as frustration. The dream ended at a dead end. Progoff has a technique for learning from dreams called "twilight imagery." Here we simply relax, letting go of all conscious thinking and entering into a state between sleep and waking. We quietly feel the atmosphere of the dream. Mr. Hart did so without success. Three times he tried, only to fail. (It is not easy to command the unconscious.) But on the fourth try, the dream imagery extended itself. Mr. Hart walked down a large hallway with a series of doors on both sides, all locked. He asked himself, "Why am I here?" Then he smelled an odor that brought him to the door of his first dream. Once again he tried to open the door, straining and struggling, pushing and pulling and tugging to no avail. Suddenly he had a feeling that someone was behind him whose arms reached up and around him and easily pushed the door open in front of him in the center. Mr. Hart concluded, "And I just went in. I didn't know who did it, but I felt that it was someone who was very friendly to me."

Force was the power that Mr. Hart, a successful business man, had displayed all his life. Yet his "scent" (meaning his intuition) guided him to a door. Another power, separate from himself and yet intimately connected with him, opened the door with ease. Mr. Hart experienced the developed dream sequence as profoundly awesome. Progoff wrote of the experience of Mr. Hart as he shared his dream with the group: "Curiously, no one in the group spoke of it as God. Perhaps that was because no one needed to."[10]

Dreams can help us uncover truth as well as cure fears and fulfill desires. Today, however, many people are suspicious of dreams or are embarrassed by believing in such "superstitions," as they call them. It is understandable to suspect what we do not know or have not experienced. It is easy to ignore our dreams, to say, "I do not dream." All of us dream, but most of us have not learned how to remember our dreams although we may dream from four to seven times each night.

I offer below suggestions for remembering and understanding dreams:

1. Have a positive attitude, knowing that you will succeed. Keep an open, unworried mind. Forget excuses.

2. Have pencil, pad, or tape recorder beside the bed.

3. Record the events of your day before going to sleep.

4. Make a conscious intent to awaken. Before going to sleep repeat, "When I dream, I will awaken and remember my dream." Relax, let go of thoughts and feelings to descend into sleep.

5. When you waken, jot down a word or two, a symbol, image, impression or feeling, or speak into the tape recorder. Then go back to sleep.

6. In the morning expand and think about your dreams and your notes; date them. Ask, "What did I see, hear, feel? How does this relate to what is happening to me at this period in my life? What was the animal, car, etc. doing? What does that tell me

about myself? What issues am I dealing with now (health, security, identity, relationships, making decisions)?"

7. Collect your dreams and get a sense of recurrent personal symbols within them, thus developing a personal dictionary of dream symbols.

8. Interpret the dream by remembering that everything and everybody in the dream represents some aspect of you. You are the center of your world within the dream. What does it mean to you? Only you can interpret your dream. Look for connections between dream images and your self-experience.

9. Pray about your dreams. Dialogue with God and be honest. Express what you are feeling, and ask God to teach you how to pray through the Spirit in order to reveal the meaning of your dreams to heal or guide or strengthen you. Ask God what God wants you to know.

To restate for emphasis: for the Christian the dream can have a divine dimension. Dreams that do so affirm the dreamer's relation to God and God's love of her or him. Dreams can convey the certainty that wherever the dreamer is, God is, and all is well.

Some people have dreams that call them to specific tasks. Whether we are awake or sleeping, God or "Someone" calls us to self-surrender. Dag Hammarskjold wrote in 1961 in *Markings:* "I don't know Who—or what—put the question, I don't know when it was put. I don't even remember answering. But at some moment I did answer Yes to Someone—or Something—and from that hour I was certain that existence is meaningful and that, therefore, my life, in self-surrender, had a goal."[11]

The healing power of dreams and of the imagination is made possible by the wealth of the unconscious mind; manifestations of it into consciousness; and the energy that flows between the two dimensions of our psyche. The unconscious conveys stored-up wisdom and hints of future possibilities. We are eager to remember them, even to risk them. We remember our dreams by discussing them with friends who will listen but not interpret. We find ourselves associating symbols, characters, or objects to dreams. They become food for meditating, praying, and journalizing. By relating thus to the dream, we offer friendship to the unconscious. We become accepting of dreaming as a way that God speaks to us.

Journal Writing

When I returned home, I listened to my telephone messages. The voice said, "Hi, this is . . . What are you doing?" That was not the entire message, but hearing those words caused me to reflect: "What *am* I doing?" and I ran for my journal. I wrote, "This is a time when . . ." and continued to write about my reflections. People have been writing down their feelings, thoughts, and experiences for a long time but for many different reasons. Here are a few that reflect the value of journal writing in the life of the spirit.

Journal writing can be a way of taking ourselves seriously. Through journalizing, we can dialogue with ourself, our body, work, society, church and family, and even with God. As we write, we learn to know ourselves better. This can lead to accepting and loving ourselves. In the process we can consciously allow "the Spirit of him who raised Jesus from the dead" to dwell in us, as Paul wrote of the Spirit's work (Romans 8:11). As we read what we have written, we see our human desires, our needs, and even the idols that take precedence over God. We too can write our confessions as Augustine did.

In addition, writing can unblock confusions, help us to discover our priorities and to make decisions, and sort out tensions and fears. By listing the pros and cons of a decision, including what bothers us and how we are feeling, we can begin to integrate the functions of feeling and thinking, thus using both.

Journalizing is creating our own sabbath. We unleash emotional and creative energy, resolve conflicts, and find new direction for life. The lack of intimacy with ourselves and consequently with others is what creates the loneliest and most alienated people in the world. The process in which a person emerges from loneliness is essentially an inward one, enhanced by journal writing.

A few years ago after I had "retired," I had to make a major decision about what I would do with the rest of my life. I was preparing to lead a group using Ira Progoff's journal method. [12] He suggests recording eight to twelve significant stepping stones in one's life, the crucial, important events that are memorable. Then after the steps have been written, the person looks for a thread that runs through them. Although I had not done this for several years,

I did so again in preparation for the class. To my amazement new events emerged, which I wrote down, events that clearly revealed the decision I needed and wanted to make but had not been aware of before the writing.

The journal can become our garbage pail. In the writing process we release emotions in a safe and constructive manner. We begin to recognize and "own" our daily experiences and our feelings. All of us need opportunities for being honest about our feelings and thoughts. Keeping a private journal can thus be therapeutic. Writing our reflections rids us of our painful feelings. Because of our naming them they may slink off into the darkness. We need to throw away these feelings. In journalizing we can do so without embarrassment or fear of offending another person.

As I was reading the other morning, the muscles in my back became tense, my stomach churned; and I felt restless. I wanted to get outside and walk far and vigorously. I felt like Job when he cried, "I am allotted months of emptiness, and nights of misery [Job 7:2]." I longed for an answer, as Job longed to speak with God. I knew that sometimes that answer, however, is silence. Sometimes the answer is "Do your own work." Perhaps I should have walked. Perhaps the body was asking for exercise. I was curious, however, to know if these feelings had any other message. I was eager to see if I could find an answer for myself. There is a saying to the effect that when there is a purpose in pain persons can survive with strength and courage. I knew that my restlessness, emptiness, and tension were messages of basic problems and conflicts I was unwilling to recognize and therefore to resolve. I also knew that many problems could not be resolved completely. Compromises with loss and pain are necessary, and life is living above and around and through obstacles. Yet I believed, and still do, that our problems can provide us with the possibilities for deepening and broadening our consciousness.

So I wrote in my journal, "I am feeling———because———." Now the work of putting emotions into words began. I am feeling empty, restless, lonely, anxious, heavy . . . but why? Then I remembered a telephone call I needed to make. (There are many ways to escape awareness.) I needed to order the book! I encountered a long-distance, cold, impersonal voice at the other end of the line, telling me I could not order it. Because I had ordered the book the previous month, I knew the woman was wrong, and I persevered. It was not pleasant. She refused to listen and kept saying no! I knew I was right because not only had I recently purchased the books, but I was their author; so I continued saying yes! I do not mean to gloat, but I am pleased that my yes won over her no. If only all yes's could do so! The call distracted my feelings of restlessness. It also suggested an answer: shift your attitude from the emptiness of no, of doubt and fear and heaviness, to the yes of trust and love and hope. As the seminary bell rang through the community to begin another day, I remembered my many blessings. The attitude of gratitude calmed the restless sea of my bodily unrest, and I remembered that heaviness crushes hope or, to put it another way, without hope there is a heaviness. Journalizing is a way of seeing into events. It can liberate the imagination.

Sometimes we are not aware of the meaning of our feelings until we write them down in the context of events. Why do I feel this way? What happened to trigger these feelings? What do they mean? How can I use them in a positive and effective way? What do they tell me about myself?

Journal writing is a way to inner listening. One way to develop a strong sense of the inner self and gradually an awareness of the spiritual power of that self is through journal writing. Spiritual journalizing requires courage and discipline. It takes courage to become aware of what needs changing in ourselves (hopes and hurts, fears and failures, lacks and losses), and it requires discipline to reflect and write for a concentrated period of time. Lives of prayer are rooted in discipline.

Writing of joy and peace are also important for those periods when we need to be reminded that "this too will pass." One of the reasons I keep a journal is that I forget. When I am tired and discouraged, I forget the times that God has revealed, in many different ways, messages of meaning. Rereading the journal feeds my hope. It is one of my ways of tasting the Father's love at the banquet.

In times of spiritual crises we can "return to Galilee," return to moments spent in Jesus' presence and in God's love. We read that Mary kept "these things" and "pondered" them in her heart. Journalizing is a way of pondering. There is no experience without reflection, no impression without expression.

Spiritual journal writing can also be a way of discovering what we truly believe. Sometimes we do not know what we think until we write it. Writing unlocks meaning. Seeing in black and white what we have experienced encourages exploration into the meaning and message of the event.

One of the greatest benefits of journalizing is discerning the providence and love of God. Journal writing uses and prods the imagination to encounter Christ and his transforming love. It is a way to reflect and reveal, to be honest before God with our questions and doubts, our emotions and thoughts. It is a place to pray.

Martin Luther, in response to his barber's request for help in prayer, told him to keep paper and pen at hand to write down what God told him. Writing it down forces us to be precise and particular, for as Luther said, the palest ink is stronger than the strongest memory. For the Christian, our journal can become the place where we record the process of our spiritual growth and journey. When we record the love we have received from God, we are blessed and energized to love others. Our journal becomes a friend, a confidant who will not give away our secrets.

To follow the stepping stones of our life in the Spirit is to heal, to make whole, by connecting apparently unrelated events, finding a path and creating the story of who we are and where we are going. Life in the Spirit means a consciously-lived relationship with God. Our goal is the kingdom, yet we are already there. For as Catherine of Siena said, "All the way to heaven is heaven."

Steps for journalizing:

1. Buy a notebook in which to record your inner journey.

2. Give it a home; that is, keep the journal with pen or pencil in the same place all the time. Choose a regular time for journalizing. I write as soon as I awake, because my mind is quiet then and more receptive to the presence of God. This may not be practical for you. But certainly when we are recording dialogues with God, or praying, it is important to become quiet and let go of tension and thinking.

3. Date the entries and number the pages. I keep an index in the back of my notebook for quick reference.

4. Reflect on the previous day's events and what one or more reveal to you.

5. Meditate on the meaning of the event(s) and write down further insights. In the beginning daily writing is important in order to establish the discipline. Choose a place where you will not be disturbed. This way of self-examination through prayer, meditation, Bible reading, reflection, and recording is revealing and private. Someone once said, "If I should die before I wake, please throw my journal in the lake."

Journal writing was part of Puritan spirituality. Prayer was a central and daily activity, and the journal writing took the place of confession to a priest. The Puritans' writings include confessions, experiences of mystical union with God, and records of answered prayer. Through the ages spiritual autobiographies by Christians have given guidance and hope to other Christians, helping them live lives of prayer and action. They can be superb guides for journalizing. When C. G. Jung was asked to write his autobiography, he undertook, in his eighty-third year, to tell his "personal myth." "I can only make direct statements, only 'tell stories,'" he wrote. "Whether or not the stories are 'true' is not the problem; the only question is whether what I tell is my fable, my truth." He said that his autobiography took a different direction than he had imagined it would at the beginning. As he wrote, he was compelled to write down his early memories. "If I neglect to do so [write] for a single day, unpleasant physical symptoms immediately follow. As soon as I set to work they vanish and my head feels perfectly clear. . . . My life has been in a sense the quintessence of what I have written, not the other way around. The way I am and the way I write are a unity. All my ideas and all my endeavors are myself. Thus the 'autobiography' is merely the dot on the i."13

There is peace and lightness when there is hope. I forget that miracles come from within. Close your eyes, and all you see is yours. There is the possibility for hope and love when there is trust, trust in God, in life, in yourself, and in others. I pass on to you, as I remember while writing in my journal, a piece of advice I was given years ago: "Do not mediate or pray for the peace and answers you feel you need until you have explored the tension within for its chaotic, creative possibilities. The tension just may be the way God is summoning your attention." Journalizing can help us see with a new inner lens and open our eyes to God's presence in all of life.

Chapter 4

The Story As Spiritual Guide

The Spiritual Guide

The role of a spiritual director or guide is not that of an expert or a taskmaster, but that of a fellow traveler and trusted friend. One who has experienced questions and doubts similar to yours, and through experience has found answers, is a welcome companion on the way to the banquet.

> Rabbi Hanokh told this story: "For a whole year I felt a longing to go to my master Rabbi Bunam and talk with him. But every time I entered the house, I felt I wasn't man enough. Once though, when I was walking across a field and weeping, I knew that I must run to the rabbi without delay. He asked: 'Why are you weeping?'
>
> "I answered: 'I am after all alive in this world, a being created with all the senses and all the limbs, but I do not know what it is I was created for and what I am good for in this world.'
>
> "'Little fool,' he replied, 'that's the same question I have carried around with me all my life. You will come and eat the evening meal with me today.'"[1]

Formalized Christian spiritual direction began with the Desert Fathers and Mothers. As we have seen, they were people who, beginning in the third century after Christ, went into the Egyptian desert in order to be more faithful and simple in the presence of

63

God. Their stories, or sayings, attest to their simple lives. But because of the harsh climate and rigorously ascetic, isolated life of the monks, their growth in prayer depended on contact with one who was wiser and more experienced. In this way, those in the desert were guided to live for God, recognizing and avoiding pitfalls and intense temptations.

Many people are unaware that they have had religious experiences. Yet religious experience is a central feature of human life. In 1963 Sir Alister Hardy, renowned British scientist, challenged his fellow scientists, in his Gifford lectures, to take religious experiences seriously. In 1969 he founded the Religious Experience Research Unit at Manchester College, Oxford. In 1977 the unit's director, Edward Robinson, conducted a study of the religious experience of childhood. He interviewed some 360 men and women, asking them to write about "any way that their lives had been affected by some power beyond themselves." He found that they recalled experiences from childhood, when they were as young as four and five, which stayed with them throughout their lives. Children, with their natural capacity of imagination, understanding, and knowing, have experiences that are essentially religious but which only in later life they can name, describe, or explain. The religious imagination, religious feelings, or the sense of the sacred are experiences lived before they are verbally expressed.

"What are the stars, Sarah?" I ask my five-year-old neighbor, before her intellect supplies her with cold, rational, unimaginative facts; and the child replies, "God's lights." "What are raindrops, Sarah?" "God's . . . God's . . . Mommy, what do you call that wet stuff in my eyes? . . . oh, God's tears."

Sarah is three years older now, but not too old to have exclaimed this summer, as we viewed the magnificent bright blue waters from Cadillac Mountain in Acadia National Park, "It's glorious!" "What are the oceans, mountains, giant redwood trees, Sarah?" "God's imagination!" Sarah has kept the wonder, the mystery, even the paradox of life in the Spirit.

Children are natural contemplatives. Because of their ability to let go, to be spontaneous, they move in and out of contemplation. Adults, having lived so long in their heads and over-used to thinking, look for results. Children enjoy experiencing with their senses, and until they experience otherwise, children trust.

At any age we may experience something "more," something that excites us and may unite us in the wonder of creation. This, perhaps the "most real" experience we will ever have, would by some be called a religious experience. For some people Jesus is their spiritual guide. For others their pastor or priest, or a trained spiritual director, provide this guidance. And still others find friends who travel with them in this spiritual capacity. Sacred stories too can be guides as they feed the spirit.

Sacred Stories

Sacred stories are food God provides at the banquet. We are hungry for meaning, for spiritual guidance, for healing and hope. The Christian story of the birth, life, death, and resurrection of Jesus of Nazareth is the core story that fashions, forms, and feeds those who are the people of the story. That story of God's dressing in flesh to dwell among us, to take off his sandals to stay awhile (at least long enough to die on a cross) called the church into being. That story feeds us by guiding, nourishing, and healing and by making life meaningful.

I recently listened to a preacher tell the story of the Israelites' wanderings in the wilderness and of their complaint to Moses for bringing them out of Egypt to die. They had no water (Exodus 17). So Moses cried out to the Lord, "What am I to do with these people? They are almost ready to stone me [TEV]." The Lord answered Moses, "Walk on ahead of the people. Take with you some of the elders of Israel and take in your hand the rod with which you struck the Nile, and go [paraphrased]."

The preacher then said, "You remember the rod." He assumed our remembrance. Do we remember the story of God's people, which is also our story? We need to remember God's story, reenacting that story, living into it, the story we will have then learned by heart. The story of the incarnation of God in Jesus is a startling revelation. It invites us toward a new perspective of ourselves and of our relationship to God and to one another. That perspective, which we call faith, is revealed through stories that correct and challenge and comfort us. These stories have a persuasive power, because they speak to the heart and head, to the emotions, as well as to the intellect.

Yet the story of the incarnation is a foolish story to many. Paul called it a "stumbling-block to Jews and folly to Gentiles [1 Cor. 1:23]," and our intellects agree. Paul wrote that we must be fools before we can be wise, "for the wisdom of the world is foolishness to God [1 Cor. 3:19, paraphrased]." Sacred stories are both foolish and full of wisdom and grab us as burrs, tenaciously. I once spent a summer reading Greek and other myths, and though they were exciting, they did not feed me as does the Christian story as told in the Gospels. It is not we who invent the sacred stories. They speak to us a word of God.

I had come to lead a workshop in storytelling, and the room was full of ministers and Christian educators eager to hear stories, eager to tell their own stories. There was not enough time, however, to hear and tell all the stories in the room. When the workshop was concluded, one woman came to me and shook my hand. "Thank you," she said. "You gave us permission to feel the story and to tell our story. I too know the power of the story." And this is the story she told me: She was a teacher, and during a lunch period one day she found herself telling an eleventh-grader how depressed and sad and shy she had felt in the eighth grade. She told him the story of how unwanted she had felt, how incompetent. And as she spoke, that teacher wondered if this student could understand what she was sharing. She did not know why she told him all that she did, but she concluded her story by saying: "I was so depressed I wanted to do away with my life. I wanted to kill myself." The boy nodded, as if he understood. The teacher smiled, touching his hand. "Now I am glad that I did not." Before she went to bed that night she again asked herself why she had told the boy her story. From where had the impetus come? Why had she told it then? She had not thought of that time of her life for many years. It had suddenly come into her consciousness and out of her mouth. She shook her head and went to sleep.

Seven years later the teacher learned from the principal that the boy had had a gun in his dresser drawer at home and that very day was planning to kill himself. When he heard her story, he had changed his mind. She smiled at me now, as she finished her story, and again took my hand. "Keep telling the story!" she said. "And keep telling us to tell our stories!"

The literature of the Spirit reminds us that our eternal values have to do with centering our lives in God rather than in achieving purposes and possessions. Sacred stories are clues, sign posts, maps to the spiritual potential of the human life. They express impossible possibilities, thus their foolishness. Such metaphors of meaning as stories contain provide us with a level of consciousness that is spiritual. Through these stories we reclothe the truth of our old traditions in the garments of current circumstances. Sacred stories are songs of the imagination. They are the way we talk about our religious encounters with God. The imagination births stories: it is the foundation, the source, of all thinking that is alive and creative.

In *The Power of Myth* Joseph Campbell tells the pygmy legend of the little boy who found in the forest a bird with a beautiful song and brought it home. But the father did not want to feed a mere bird and so he killed it. And with the bird, he killed the song, and with the song, himself. [2]

Out sacred stories feed our faith also. Faith is believing beyond belief. The Bible is too sacred to be true, for in its stories we encounter God. It is the story that feeds us *beyond* belief. Yet, tragically, much of our time is spent in attempting to intellectualize faith. Horace Bushnell, raised by religious parents in a nineteenth-century New England Congregational church, at age seventeen experienced a deep religious conversion. By the time he reached Yale College, however, his doubts had grown and his religious fervor had dimmed. Upon graduation he went from being a journalist to a lawyer, all the time trying to intellectualize his faith. When he returned to Yale to teach, he was tormented by doubts and finally realized that he had substituted thought for other life experiences in his attempts to create a religion of the head. Recognizing his dependence upon God, he prayed, vowing to trust as he had never trusted before. The result was a sense of faith, the release of doubt, and the decision to enter the ministry. Bushnell describes this as his true conversion to Christian life and faith.

An intellectualized faith deceives us into a false sense of independence from God. The intellect, relied upon alone, will serve to separate us from a deep, sustaining relationship with God. Rationality severs trust in God, which is the meaning of faith. Facts can take us only so far. When Albert Einstein was asked to explain his theories of relativity, he declined to do so but instead invited the questioner to his home to hear Mozart. And when Paul Tillich was confronted by his seminary students' agonizing doubts and despairs, he played the Credo from Bach's B Minor Mass for them.

Theology is a garment of God, pointing to God. Jesus once said, "Except you become as a little child [unless you allow the child within you life and begin to trust and love and wonder as a child] you cannot enter the kingdom of heaven [Matt. 18:3, paraphrased]." Wonder is an opening to God, an awareness that there is spiritual as well as physical life. Without a spiritual life we are alienated from the rest of life. But perhaps we have alienated ourselves from wonder and from nature, which can make us full of wonder. We may have narrowed our understanding, blown out our imagination, stamped down our feelings, all in exchange for the rational, intellectual process. To be dominated by the intellect is to be protected from experience. The primitive called this "loss of soul." Jung called his patients "lost sheep," people who had lost their faith. Those who take a rigid view of religion or scientific truth have lost their soul, their sense of play, their capacity to wonder, their ability to appreciate and imagine.

James Fowler, author of *Stages of Faith,* once told of becoming dried up and needing help. He went to a Jesuit spiritual director who told him to meditate for three days with the story of the feeding of the five thousand. The first day he was to read and reread the story until he mastered its details. The second day he was to visualize himself in the story, using his senses to smell and listen, taste and touch and look. The third day he was to encourage his mind to play with the story in his own life. He discovered that image meeting image in his imagination could be an instrument of the Spirit. "I got in touch with my needs, with my hungers. I found a vulnerability. And I found a mediator. All this was in a way that I had not found from using my cognitive approach."[3] Fowler had found the unconscious-producing symbols that can depict a person's needs, challenges, and directional tendencies. Affective education through the story that speaks to the emotions, or the heart, as well as to the head, initiates one into the depths and heights of human experience, where we trust in God's love, living life in the Spirit.

Faith is the light that illumines how we see and what we see. An old Russian tale tells of a father who had three sons. Two thought themselves very clever, and the third everyone thought to be a fool. The father built a small hut on the edge of his land and called his sons together to give it to one of them, saying, "To the one of you who can fill this hut completely I will give this hut as a prize. But remember, not a corner must be left empty." The oldest son, very clever, had an immediate solution and ran into town to buy a horse. Alas, the horse filled only one corner of the hut. The second son then ran to town with, he thought, an even cleverer idea. He returned with a load of hay, but it, too, filled only a part of the hut.

The third son, as he was simple, was not so quick to come to a solution. He wandered the whole day trying to think of what would fill the hut without leaving an empty corner. As night fell, he slipped into town, still without a clever idea. Only one thing distracted his thoughts, the lights coming from the town homes. That was it! Quickly he bought a candle and brought it back to the hut where he lit it. He filled the hut, every corner, with light. And the hut was his!

When faith fills our hut, our lives, we are sustained. Sacred stories are lights on our path and food for our spirit. When Israel was carried off into captivity, the psalmist sang, "How can I sing the Lord's song in a strange land?" Yet while the other small nations were gobbled up by Babylon, Israel survived because the story she took with her survived and gave survival power to the people.

Many times sacred stories use symbolic language that presents opposites and contradictions. Sacred stories therefore are comfortable with ambiguity and both/and resolutions. They help us live life that is itself paradoxical. The story does this because it describes; it does not define. Theologizing is talking *about* God. Storytelling is *experiencing* God in and through the word. The story does not solve a contradiction but presents and remains within the paradox in peace. The story knows the paradox is never fully solved, for its solution is secret, God's secret.

Long ago I heard an old Hasidic story. It goes like this. When a child is conceived, God whispers to that child the secrets of the universe. Then the child in the womb hears God's stories, stories of God's calling into existence the sun and moon and stars, separating the land from the waters, and creating rainbows and relationships. For nine months God reveals what there is to know of creation; then the child is ready to be born. In the excitement and joy of being born, of entering the world, however, the child forgets all the secrets, even the secret of God's love and presence; and the rest of the child's life is spent searching for those secrets once again.

Sometimes a story tiptoes in and whispers in our ear in sickness, fear, and worry: "Lean back. Rest. Let me carry you for awhile." And we forget ourselves, our aches and pains, our disappointments. Sometimes it says, "Go and do likewise"; other times, "Eat, this is the story that was given for you."

The Parable Reveals the Spirit

The solution of life is a secret and will never be guessed until it is revealed. Life in the Spirit is discovering that secret in the story of Jesus, the Christ, the Parable of God. Parables are stories that challenge us and correct us indirectly. When Nathan told King David the story of the rich man who took the poor man's one lamb, he was speaking of David's stealing Uriah's wife, Bathsheba (2 Samuel 12:1–15). The story spoke for Nathan's judgment, and David heard. Preaching on adultery would have brought forth rational excuses from the king. Defensively David would not have heard, "You are the man!"

The word *parable* comes from the Greek word *parabole*. It is a juxtaposition for the sake of comparison. It involves the uniting of an abstract declaration or demand, concept or fact, with a vivid story or situation. The difference between an allegory and a parable is that in the allegory each thing stands for a value, principle, or moral. By contrast in the parable the whole story is the representation. Parables picture precepts, persons, and paradoxes upon the mind's eye.

Jesus used parables to reveal spiritual dimensions. He used

ordinary objects and familiar experiences in new and extraordinary ways. In telling his parables, which were his metaphors for the rule of God, he brought new meaning to the old and ordinary so that his hearers might see the presence of God in their midst. In Jesus' parables, he allows room for God to be transcendent. The people came to the telling of Jesus' stories with their own perceptions, creeds, and dogmas, their answers to life's questions. But Jesus took their preconceptions and tossed them into the air. He did this so that God's transcendence could enter and the Spirit transform the people from respondents with rigid answers to persons with flexible, living, dynamic ones.

Most of us must live with reasonable or rational answers that we use to control our environment. We can stand only so much chaos. There is anguish in standing before the silence of Mystery. To find meaning in our suffering, to make it endurable, we are given partial answers. The nurse who suffers over the children dying before her eyes prays, "God, why do you permit this? Why don't you do something?" God, first silent, replies, "I did something. I made you." Four friends brought the lame man to Jesus. Perhaps the sufferer could not believe he would be cured, so his friends carried him to Jesus because of their faith.

Jesus' parables gave God room to act, to surprise people, to be transcendent. Jesus' stories introduced paradox: security comes from insecurity; possessions accrue from lack of ownership; and— the greatest embarrassment of all, the folly of the cross—Jesus' defeat and ignominy was not a rejection by God but an exultation of God. Perhaps it was the supreme parable. Jesus, who died as one who told parables of God, arose the Parable of God.

The parables are comparisons. Jesus used the symbol, the metaphor, because he was speaking of the Unknown. He helped us understand the unfamiliar by comparing it to the familiar: "It is like yeast which a woman took and mixed with half a hundredweight of flour till it was all leavened [Luke 13:20–21; Matt. 13:33, paraphrased]." In Jesus' world leaven was a familiar item. Although it was a little thing, such as a grain or a seed, it was powerful in its activity and essential to the making of bread, the staple of the people's lives. In our day of bakeries, of frozen and fast foods, few people bake their own bread. But the metaphor is still provocative and telling. Jesus used leaven as an image for spiritual reality, a reality experienced and felt, rather than completely understood. This reality can penetrate the whole person, through and through, as leaven does bread.

The predominant themes of Jesus' parables are that the reign of God is at hand. Also God's love is for all, in particular for the poor, the oppressed, the outcast and distressed, those who are in need. The reign of God precipitates a crisis of decision. It demands a response by word and deed.

As Christians we have a story to tell. Because of the importance of its message, we wish to tell it as effectively as we can. Parable is implicit communication of a concept or a truth. Thus it has both a literal and a figurative meaning.

Symbolic Language

Writing about stories, about parables, however, is like interpreting stories. When we let the story speak through its symbolic language in the telling or reading, the Spirit speaks through the story, breathing into us its message, its sustenance. Stories use symbolic language, which is their power. Truth is a living reality, captured only in the moment of experiencing. So, what is the place of interpretation? Because a story is a symbol, it not only represents but has its own meaning as an energy or a message. We look at a traffic sign, and it is simply a sign to stop or go. But we can enter into the experience of it as a symbol. We then participate in its message. It is charged with emotions, and we bring our emotions to it. A story, like a symbol, has a power and an energy to re-create what has gone before. It preserves the memory in a manner that makes meaning for the one who hears (or reads) it and especially for the one who tells it.

Stories as symbols have personal meanings. They remind us of our own stories. Each of us has his or her own stories for living in the dark. The Revelation of John is an example of such a story. It is an apocalypse written for persecuted Christians, to give them hope and light for their darkened day. It has power to make sense out of the chaos of existence, for it can grasp the hearer at the level of feeling and intuition. Story is an imaginative way of ordering experience.

Recently I heard a minister with intense sensitivity and complete immersion in the biblical words read the story of the Book of Revelation. She did more than read the words; she *was* the word. As the story unfolded before our eyes and ears in the darkened chapel, John began his revelation: "Blessed is the one who reads aloud the words of the prophecy." The Book of Revelation was meant to be told. There was power and energy in the preacher's words. John would have been proud, for the words were lifted from the page and given life, sound, and movement. We not only heard but we saw and tasted. We were at the banquet feast and the words fed us: *angel, throne, scroll, lamb, horse and rider, bowl of blood, woman in scarlet, dragon, beast from the sea, a new heaven, a new earth, river of the water of life, the tree of life, the holy city.*

God created out of the Word, and there was creative energy in the minister's words. We felt power and potency, as the words trembled and shook and shone as sunlight upon the golden throne. In the darkness the words comforted and healed us as the river of the water of life. "And the Word was with God, the light shining in the darkness. The Word became flesh and we saw his glory, full of grace and truth." And when she spoke her final words, "Come, Lord Jesus!" he came, as he comes over and over in the word, in the sacred stories. Such stories are manna from heaven, food for the spirit, bread for the banquet. They feed us hope and healing, invite us into wholeness. Sacred stories restore the original power of the word. Isaiah wrote that the word of God goes forth and will not return until it accomplishes its end. Narrative theology presents paradox, ambiguity, and symbolic images of meaning and hope. The sacred story by which we live and make meaning is a living story, a way of encountering God and hope.

The art of theology is telling about and listening to "those stories" of which John writes ("These are written that you may believe [Rev. 20:31]"). The art of storytelling is tasting and experiencing those stories, living with them until they transform our thinking and our actions. Sacred stories can shift the center of our awareness from self-consciousness to self-surrender. Some of them can even bring us out of bondage into the freedom of God's presence and love.

If the function of story, parable, and myth is to reveal, to open up, or to disclose, then the symbols embedded in them are the interpretation, expressing something unexplainable in any other way. Therefore, interpreting the story can rob it of some of its power. The power of the story is dissected the minute we question or interpret it. Then we stop experiencing the story and enter the world of abstraction. The story must speak for itself. When the people asked Jesus what the story meant, he told them another story. Symbolic language is personal. The interpreter of a story cannot tell others what that story means to them. Each person is unique—with his and her own experiences, expectations, needs, and desires—and thus hears the story differently from others.

The power of the story is released through the imagination in its listener and reader. Genuine stories are always primary sources of power. Interpretation clothes them in the fashion of the day, but the naked story lives on, its truth never exhausted, its verbal imagery defying conceptualization, while offering us a lived-in experience and allowing the mystery and numinosity to shine.

Children experience story in this way. While I was reading the *Narnia Chronicles* to my seven-year-old granddaughter, she said, "It seems like you're going into it [Narnia] when you read it." When Charles's sister, Sarah, seven, complained, "I like television better than reading, Mommy. In reading you can't see the pictures," Charles, nine, put it this way: "Yes, you can, Sarah. You can see your own pictures, only clearer. Mom reads and after awhile you hear them talking. It's like going into a trance."

So we see that the story resists interpretation while at the same time inviting it. Stories cannot tolerate bodiless minds nor mind-less bodies. In story we see wholly; feeling and thinking and interpreting. However, while the meaning is individual new meanings, insights, inner riches can be revealed through shared interpretation. Without interpretation we have money in the vault but no key to open it, especially if the story is so far from the hearer's comprehension that it may be ignored or dismissed. Unless we reflect, meditate, and ponder the images to deepen the experience of the story, it can fly out of the head as quickly as it flew in.

Yet, too much interpretation will rob the story of its power and separate the hearers from it. With too little interpretation some stories are inaccessible to us, clothed in ancient, cultural garb. I have seen stories shine more clearly, be opened up to cast light where before there had been darkness, through inspired, informed interpretation. Both intuition and knowledge are useful. The question is: Will this interpretation open up or close down the story? The story is neither truth, which is abstract, nor direct experience, which is bound to the particular. It lives symbolically, presenting truth and meaning, healing and hope, food for life in the Spirit. Jesus answered Pilate's question "What is truth?" by standing before him.

The Meaning of Myth

The meaning of our life and its renewal are dependent on our faith symbols and stories. John wrote at the end of his Gospel, "These [stories] are written so that you may believe that Jesus is the Christ, the Son of God, and that believing you may have life in his name [20:31]." Men and women are hungry for meaning. Meaninglessness inhibits the fullness of life and has the power to make us ill.

We have heard of people in concentration camps, prisons, and solitary confinement who survived extreme torture and deprivation because they had stories in their heads, stories they had memorized or stories they created out of their own vivid imaginations—"good stories," as children would call them. These stories helped them see meaning in their suffering.

Recently a friend of mine had a conversation with her seven-year-old son as he anticipated Christmas. "It is fun to think about things ahead," he said, "but I like to think about good things that have happened." With his mother listening, the boy continued, "You know, sometimes bad things can happen. You can die. You and Dad can get a divorce. It is scary, so I just like to think about good things that have happened because they are safe." We call such "good things" stories of hope and healing and wholeness. Some stories feed us deeply and corporately, especially the stories we call myth. Myth is a story that shows, as well as tells, a truth that can be expressed in no other way. "Myth" has been used to mean untruthfulness, but actually myth is the way truth is revealed. Myth conveys mystery and the sacred. Myths—those large stories by which whole groups of people know who they are—can feed a person's hope and make meaning out of chaos. They construct images of hope and trust and love as foundations for new perspectives.

The twentieth-century writer Laurens Van der Post grew up in Africa. At one time in his life he lived with the Bushmen of the Kalahari Desert, recorded their stories, and experienced their life. In doing so he felt a sense of meaning he had never had before, which rejuvenated his own cultural heritage. For him it made the biblical story clearer and gave it a new energy that it had never had. He found that the Bushman lived in extraordinary intimacy with nature. They belonged; they felt known. Our scientific knowledge has possibly blocked us from a sense of belonging to nature, from the sense of being known by the natural world and of knowing it. Western men and women learn in order to control, rather than to love, to be known "as we are known." The Bushman looks at the stars and speak of "Grandmother Sirius," of "Grandfather Canis." The psalmist too sang of God's naming the stars. The supreme experience of the primitive spirit is in his or her stories. The story was a most sacred possession. Van der Post wrote: "He knew intuitively that without a story one had no clan or family; without a story of stories, no life-giving continuity with the beginning and therefore no future. Life for him was living a story."

In his chapter "Homesick for a Story" from *The Heart of the Hunter,* Van der Post tells of Hhabbo, the old Bushman who described his emotions about the story. Hhabbo is the Bushman name for "dream." Dream was in prison, sentenced to the hardest possible labor on the breakwater in Table Bay because when hungry he had killed a springbuck of the veld on the property of a man who had stolen all his land. Dream said, "Master, thou knowest that I sit waiting for the moon to turn back for me, that I may return to my place; that I may listen again to all the people's stories. For [when] I am here, I do not obtain stories." Dream told of his fellow Bushmen listening to the stories, and how he would sit and watch for a story, waiting for it to float into his ear. Though there might be mountains between and though the road was long, the story would come floating to him. Listening, he would feel in his ear the story that is in the wind. More than being homesick for his place or for his people, Dream was homesick for his story.[4]

The Bushman had a story about everything. The late Ken Feit, whose story introduced chapter 1 of this volume, traveled about the world gathering stories and "enfleshing" them. He told the story of hare and moon that Van der Post recorded in the *Heart of the Hunter.* Feit heard the story many years after Van der Post, when he was in Africa. It is the story "The Message of Moon": Moon had a message for man and woman, and called Insect to come and carry the message to earth. The message of Moon was this: "As I die and in dying, live, so you in dying will live also." Insect took the message of Moon to earth and on the way met Hare. "Where are you going?" asked Hare.

"I have a message from Moon to man and woman. Moon said 'As I die and in dying, live again, so you in dying will live also.'"

"Insect, you are so slow. Let me take it," said Hare, and Insect gave the message to Hare.

Hare ran off. When he found man and woman, in his hurry he said, "Moon has sent you a message that in dying, Moon dies; so you too in dying shall perish." When Moon heard what Hare had said, Moon was angry and took a stick and hit Hare on the nose. And that is why hares have split noses and why men and women think that when they die they perish.

To speak to the world as "Thou" is to see it spiritually and relate to it imaginatively. To relate to the world from one's story may not be logical, but if I must give up part of my logic for the sake of my healing, that is a small price to pay. The purpose of Jesus' healing and teaching was to announce the coming of the rule of God that in Jesus is already here. That means to me that God rules the physical and the spiritual, the political and the social, the individual and the communal, the conscious and the unconscious. To express this we stutter in symbols. Some symbols throw a light. Others confuse. Their function is not so much to help us understand but to help us "stand under" these wide paradoxes, the mystery of our reality.

God feeds us through the story. It is the task of the story to help us imagine. Let me give you an example. I have a problem. I am angry. I think. I become logical and rational, and I tell my feelings to keep quiet. But the problem becomes larger, it consumes my thinking. At last in desperation, I cry, "Jesus, help me! What is the answer?" At this point in my frustration, I remember the Desert Fathers' story "Careless," which has had meaning for me (see chapter 1). Thus, to my incredulity Jesus replies by giving me a memory of a story. It is not my reply, for it is a surprise. Stories are one of the ways God speaks to us and remind us of God's power.

The following is an old story. I do not even remember where I heard it first: The man, weary with living, disenchanted with life, burdened with boredom, suffering, and struggling to find meaning, set out for Paradise, the place of his dreams, where all would be perfect.

He walked all day, energized by the excitement of his quest, the desire of his dream. By dusk he had reached a dark forest, where he sat down and ate his supper of a crust of hard bread and a drink of warm water. Then having said his prayers, the man placed his shoes in the path facing the direction he would walk again the next morning. While he slept and dreamed of Paradise, a trickster came along the path and reversed the direction of the shoes, pointing them toward the place from which the poor man had come.

The next morning he arose with vigor, ready to reach his destination. He thanked the Creator of the Universe for the glory of the day, put on his shoes, and began walking. He walked all that day with a song in his heart and a skip to his step, for after all, he thought he was on the way to Paradise. All that day he walked as if in a dream and at dusk reached The City. The setting sun was shining golden on the leaves of the trees, covering the roofs of the houses with a fiery red; and though the city looked familiar and was not as large as he had expected Paradise to be, he entered with a light heart and a soft step. He followed his feet to a familiar door where a familiar family greeted him with warmth and joy. And there he lived happily everafter, for he was at last in Paradise.

Jesus said, "The kingdom of God, what shall I compare it with?" and told a story. So the story makes meaning, presents truth, the truth you find and give to what you hear and see and experience as you live life in the Spirit. Some people call faith a perspective, a way of seeing reality. Stories can give us a new perspective, for we choose how we perceive.

Gaining a New Perspective Through Stories

Paul wrote, "Do not conform any longer to the pattern of this world, but be transformed by the renewing of your mind [Rom. 12:2, paraphrased]." Perspective plays an important part in who we are and how we respond to the conditions in which we live. We choose how we perceive, and that choosing is a matter of life and death.

Three groups of rats were given a series of electrical shocks: one group could escape, one group could not escape, and the third group was given no shocks at all. Twenty-four hours later, after the rats were reexposed to the shocks, their immune function was tested. It was significantly inhibited in the group with no escape and not inhibited in the group with an escape. The conclusion is that the link between psychological factors and disease is in the amount of control the rats saw they had. The immune system was altered by "learned helplessness." Similarly, researchers testing the saliva of students taking an exam found that A, or IgA, a protein that protects against viruses of the upper respiratory tract, dropped most in students who needed to control and be in power. Stress lowers resistance to infection so that we actualize our fears, becoming that which we fear most.

Stories can help us transform our perspectives of reality. When we experience a sense of God's love through participating in stories that permeate us by providing inner power and external purpose, we experience a sense of well-being and confidence. To be content, to see life as our wish come true, affects who we are. After Jesus first touched the blind man's eyes, the man saw persons as trees walking, but on the second touch, the dimness was removed; he was transformed. Sometimes our perceptions need a second touch to open our eyes to the wonders and works of God among us. Sacred stories help us to see.

Stories and Healing

A living myth has the power to heal. Today we are beginning to recognize that technological answers and understanding will not save us, despite what Madison Avenue, the Pentagon, and industry would have us believe. We have to rely on our intuition, our real being. This is not to deny reason. But we must face and overcome the dark passions, the irrational savage within us all to then discover there the resources of character to meet our destiny and the power to serve others.

The entire sacred story as recorded in scripture is the story of God's saving acts, the outpouring of divine love, a tender, compassionate, caring love. God is interested in forgiveness and healing. When we confess, Jesus says, "I know that and I love you." God yearns for our wholeness, our trust in his love, which relinquishes our fears of him, so that we may be healed. A young man had had a great fear of lightning all his life. Forced to walk through a storm during the night to seek help for a camping companion who had become violently ill, he was grateful for the aid of his flashlight. As the storm grew worse, a sudden bolt of lightning caused him to drop and break the flashlight. Almost numb with fear, he felt helpless. He could not move. But with the next flash of lightning he found that he could see, and a calm settled over him. He realized that the lightning, which he had so long feared, was helping him overcome a seemingly impossible situation.

Encountering God in the spiritual heart, where love and trust are home, releases us from the chains that bind us. Bad experiences from the past, anxieties and fears for the future, the need for control or the clinging to people and possessions—all are chains that separate us from God.

Healing is saying yes to the life of the Spirit, and hope is a healing fact. It cures the restlessness, the boredom, the despair we experience. The words of a story can heal and comfort. Sometimes, however, the story must challenge and correct before it can heal. Through stories we can face the images and ideas that frighten us and seek their cause and meaning in order to grow into real freedom.

A friend, who was an adviser to a group of youth, asked them to choose, from pictures she had displayed on a floor, one that showed their relationship with God now. They were then to share with the group the reason they chose it. One of the young men, when it was his turn to speak, stood up to show his picture. He had chosen a picture of a purple hippopotamus in tennis shoes on a ladder, painting. He explained: "I have always done what my parents told me. I have been a good boy. This picture shows my relationship to God right now. Hippos are not purple. They do not wear tennis shoes, or climb ladders, or paint. Like this hippo, I am a fake." The young man's voice shook as he spoke, and he began to cry. The others surrounded him with hugs and tears, and one of them prayed aloud.

Stories of Quests

Out of our longing for God and our hunger for spiritual food, we are called to go questing. Stories of quests are vicarious experiences that, among other things, feed our appetites for adventure. But the quest begins when we sense that something is missing. There is a sense of emptiness or disharmony, a lack of satisfaction in the way we are living. For me it was the discovery of my need to move from dependency and obedience to self-authority based on my own experience and judgment. The people on whom I had depended were no longer with me so that the old rules no longer applied. Like Jonah, I had been swallowed by the whale or, as Thomas Merton put it, I was in the "belly of a paradox."

The call to the quest is the awakening of the self. The familiar, comfortable, traditional patterns break apart. We are called to risk, to change, to grow. For the new to be born, the old must die. The biblical stories of Abraham, Joseph, Moses, Ruth, Esther, Daniel, Mary, Samson, Peter, Paul, and others are stories of quests: men and women risking their lives on their faith journeys, dynamic, enterprising, foolhardy people doing hazardous, courageous, faithful acts. So too the stories of the saints are stories of quests.

Edward Hays tells of a contemporary St. George on a spiritual journey and of his inner spiritual guide who took the form of a Chinese dragon, whom he called Igor. Igor titled George "St."; the abbreviation can represent the four-letter word "sent," indicating to us that one needs to be sent on a quest before one becomes a saint. George was not a saint, but deep within himself he felt the call to go on a holy quest. His wife was outraged, his boss suggested therapy, and his friends shook their heads in disbelief.

Then one night George went to the garage to be alone. The garage became his hermitage, a place of silence, and the place where Igor visited him. Here Igor answered George's questions with stories. Here George thought about the stories he had heard. Here he was given mystical equipment for the quest: an antique mirror and a bag of books. Here George learned to be alone. (Learning to be alone is to learn to see inside, to taste one's lack of power and self-sufficiency. Recall, in contrast, the story of the man who consulted Jung, who was afraid to be by himself.) George also learned to look into the mirror to see what was there.

It was not easy to become aware, to learn to love, but love had sent George on the quest, and love would be his goal. Igor, the dragon, told George stories that showed him how to be a good husband and a good father; and George became more patient, more relaxed, more peaceful. He wondered what would happen if the God-seed inside him would be cracked open and all the energy released as well.

Gradually George began to tell Igor's stories to Martha, his wife. These stories mapped George's spiritual journey. And each Saturday after his first Saturday of quest he spent the day in his garage to exercise and feed and push his soul to the outer limits of its possibilities. He grew comfortable with silence. Yet there were times when he felt the frustration of his feeble attempts to communicate with the Divine Mystery. It was then that his inabilities came to the surface, and he wondered why he was wasting his time. Little by little the Saturday lifestyle became a habit and the garage time, important. Because of it, he saw more clearly into the dark corners of his consciousness. In the wonderland of his imagination, in the magic theater of his mind, Igor's stories revealed what had been hidden from George's view for many years.

George fasted, prayed, and spent time in solitude. He studied the great holy books and puzzled over the parables; he wondered what more was necessary. He was eager to continue his quest, but the dragon asked him if he knew the cost of such a trip to the Land of No Limits, no limits to love. Such a quest meant George must be stripped of all possessions, even his title, name, and reputation, everything that he held dear. But the last requisite was the most foolish of all—George was to bring not only *his* garbage but the garbage of the neighborhood, that is, the filth and slime of the sins of the world.

At last George made his last entry in his journal before taking the journey with Igor. As he was going he saw Martha as if for the first time and realized what made up a real feast. Though the ingredients are only a sip of wine and a morsel of bread, if the food is flooded with love, it is truly a heavenly banquet. George was drunk with gratitude. He felt as if he had been reborn, newly alive and free! When Igor arrived, George was ready, for his passionate seeking was the major work of the quest. It was time to go. "Don't forget this," Igor said, handing the mystic mirror to George. "You may be naked as a newborn, but you'll need this." As George looked into the mirror, he remembered his first fears upon seeing his own darkness. Now that he was bearing the darkness and weakness of vast multitudes, he could look at that darkness in the mirror and say, "I love you."

"Turn it over, George, and look in the other side," Igor advised. When George turned the mirror, there was the brilliance of ten thousand sunrises, and in the center a golden chalice appeared— the Holy Grail!

"Yes, George," said a voice that came from everywhere. "Thou art that. You, George, are the Holy Grail!"[5]

The quest of the hero and heroine, small and powerless, searching, seeking, ends in the process of finding the self, the most exciting and fearful and fulfilling adventure of all. The stories of quests are symbolic of many processes: leaving home; the rite of passage; crossing the threshold of transformation; radical, painful change; death itself or the dying of former attitudes and attachments; self-surrender in order to be reborn and to return.

Before C. S. Lewis became a Christian, he loved the lore of myth but yet considered myths lies and therefore worthless, even though they "breathed through silver." His friend, and author of *The Fellowship of the Ring*, J. R. R. Tolkien refuted Lewis by arguing that as we come from God, it is from God we draw our ultimate ideas. Our imaginative inventions such as myths originate with God and therefore reflect something of eternal truth; thus they fulfill God's purpose.

Lewis responded that he found Christianity irrelevant. How could the death and resurrection of Christ "save the world"? Again Tolkien responded that although God is revealed through the minds of the poets of non-Christian myths, in the Christian story God *became* the Poet, using real people and actual history. The dying god myth found in many cultures had now taken place in history. The myth (*myth* used as earlier as a positive word for a cultural system of meaning and beliefs) became a fact. Tolkien wondered, could not he, Lewis, accept the story as food for the spirit, for if God is mythopoeic (myth making), we being made in the image of God must become mythopoeic.

The conversation between them continued until 3:00 A.M.,

when Tolkien had to go home. Now came the tough work for
Lewis. The true myth, which was nevertheless a myth, was
imaginative but illogical. Christianity required the leap of faith.
On Christmas Day, 1931, Lewis became a Christian. Although he
often questioned how he could ever have come to believe this
"cock and bull story," Paul's "stumbling block," Lewis said that one
who fed on the Christian story as myth was perhaps more
spiritually alive than one who believed the story as "fact" and did
not give it much thought.[6]

So we go on with the journey, the sacred journey we have
begun, for someone always has to carry on the story and carry the
story on. But one day we discover we have arrived. The food we
seek is spread before us. The banquet is ready and Jesus says, "This
is the story of my body as bread given for you. Come eat!"

Chapter 5

Creation Spirituality

The Feast of Creation

Aristotle said that if God were not in all things, nature would
not function. God is in the bread, the very bread with which God
feeds us at the banquet of life. God gives us the gift of nature and
we name her Mother Earth. The psalmist sang, "The earth is the
Lord's, and everything in it."

Many people find renewal and strength from being in the
presence of Mother Earth. A few years ago I left my home of
twenty-six years to live far away for a year in two small rooms.
There were times I felt confined and lonely. I had, however,
discovered that when I experienced confinement or loneliness
nature could heal. A few miles from my rooms I found a large
camping ground with a river and swiftly flowing streams. When I
arrived in August, it welcomed me under its leafy trees. In the fall,
the leaves turned scarlet and orange and filled the sky and ground
with their bounteous color. In the winter I walked in the snow and
watched the streams, listening to their murmur as they trickled
through their icy layer, soothing my spirit. In the spring the river's
riotious sounds of noisy birds and laughing children caused me to
rejoice. The park had become one of my best friends, and I was
grateful to be a partner with a part of God's creation. We do well to
allow nature to be our friend, to love her, to cherish her, to defend
her in sickness and in health until death do us part.

Now I have moved to an area of rolling green hills and white
Amish barns. There is a peace here that flows from these farms and
fields. Driving in the country revives my spirit and feeds my soul.
To walk in a park and see parables in particular leaves, flowers,

trees, birds, and squirrels is to pray. Mother Earth provides refreshment and healing for the spirit. Mother Earth comforts us in her lap. She stimulates our senses. A philosopher asked St. Anthony: "Father, how can you be enthusiastic when the comfort of books has been taken away from you?" He replied: "My book, O Philosopher, is the nature of created things, and whenever I want to read the word of God, it is usually right in front of me."[1]

In the sacred book of Islam, the Koran, Allah asks: "The heaven and the earth and all in between, thinkest thou I made them in jest?" God did not create the world in jest but in great imagination. Consider foraminifera, whose calcareous shells eventually drifted to the floor of the ocean to change into chalk and rose as the chalk cliffs of England yet whose particles are so minute that one gram of sand may contain 50,000 shells. Or consider nummulites which, converted into limestone, created the stone of the great pyramids of Egypt. Each species (and we share this planet with at least 10 million other species of living things) by being true to itself, to its unique gift, its own function, is unified with everything else.

Lewis Thomas reported going to the zoo one day where he saw a group of otters and beavers in action. His active imagination drew him into amazement at the perfection he was witnessing. "I wanted no part of the science of beavers and otters. . . . I came away from the zoo with something, a piece of news about myself . . . a surprised affection: Left to ourselves, mechanistic and autonomic, we hanker for friends."[2]

The Hasidic masters knew the grandeur and holiness of nature. They spoke of walking across the fields with their minds pure and holy. Then the sparks of soul from the stones and all growing things and all animals—bearing the holy fire—came out and clung to them. Then they were purified. Mother Earth was not created in jest but in beauty and holiness.

To see nature as God's grandeur we must become aware, open our eyes. Nature calls for a sense of waiting. We must stalk nature, much as one stalks God, both patiently waiting and banging on the door with persistence and passion, for nature is alive. Nature is alive with seashells and fallen stars, and all we need are the eyes and wonder with which to see. Gerard Manley Hopkins saw it and wrote:

The world is charged with the grandeur of God.
It will flame out, like shining from shook foil;
. . . .
There lives the dearest freshness deep down things.[3]

As I sat in the backyard looking at the stars one night with my dear friend Sarah—Sarah was four—she saw it and said: "The Emperor-of-the-world made us a good place to live." Children's inborn sense of wonder sees the oneness with nature. Is it possible to extend ourselves beyond the limited circles of family, country, and race, to discover that the only truly natural and real human unit is the spirit of the Earth?

The universe is alive with inexhaustible radiant energy. Creation is the sign language of God. The cosmos is not a realm of necessity but of free spirit, patterned on the surface, whose primary trait is spontaneity. Both the Earth and its inhabitants break the deterministic, materialistic, developmental laws of earlier science. Today science disowns any rigid theory of causality. Nature is unpredictable. The world at its core is God's Loving Will.

We are organs of one another, members of one body, as Paul wrote, living cells in one body of humankind. We are not alone in our longing and in our waiting. "The whole creation waits with eager longing. . . . The creation itself will be set free from its bondage to decay, and obtain the glorious liberty of God's children [Rom. 8:19–21, paraphrased]." All the singing, dancing stars and sun and galaxies will one day join in the new heaven and the new earth pictured in Revelation. But while we are waiting for perfection, let us do the possible and be faithful to our stewardship of Mother Earth.

The universe was not made in jest but in solemn incomprehensible earnest by a power that is unfathomably secret and holy. There is nothing to be done about it. We either ignore it or see. And then we walk fearlessly, eating what we must . . . And with the British evangelist Billy Bray we say, "I go my way, and my left foot says 'Glory,' and my right foot says 'Amen': in and out of Shadow Creek, upstream and down, exultant, in a daze, dancing to the twin silver trumpets of praise."[4]

Care and Commitment to Mother Earth

As long as Mother Earth has a lap, she can continue to comfort. But we are polluting her waters, cutting down her trees, removing her mountains, cementing her land. She has taken care of her children for millennia, and yet her children exploit her care, impoverish her soil, strip her of her forests, and pollute her skies in the name of profit. National forests and wilderness areas are being destroyed, threatening insects, fish, and birds with extinction. Air is polluted with pesticides, carbon monoxide from automobiles, sulfur dioxide from industry, and radioactive particles from power plants. In the United States four billion tons of topsoil are lost every year. When we deplete the resources of our environment, we deplete ourselves. When we cover the earth with cement, noise, and overcrowding, we gamble with our psychic well-being. Mother Earth is our origin. She nourishes and supports us. In harming her we harm ourselves. In ruining the earth we destroy ourselves, for we are earthlings. It is imperative to be passionate for her survival. To be healed we invite all of Earth's creatures to the banquet. The earth is hurting, her foundations are shaking.

For the first time in the history of creation we are destroying the life support systems of Mother Earth. Not only does our nation and the world witness the exploitation of natural resources, the use of military forces to obtain coal and uranium, global warming, acid rain, soil erosion, and toxic chemicals, but the eradication of species as well. In the next three decades it is estimated that one hundred species per day will be driven to extinction.

Tropical forests are homes for 50 to 80 percent of the plant species, and areas the size of football fields are being burned or cut every second of the day. Yet, hungry villagers of the Third World will plant crops on river banks and increase erosion and cut down too many trees for firewood, because what matters to the poor is not long-term damage to the environment but short-term survival.

Mother Earth is mother to all. It will require the whole economic system of the planet, the total human community, not only the rich and strong, to create justice and peace, compassion and care for the future of the Earth. Perhaps we in the Christian community will hear with new ears John's words to the multitudes' questions, "What then shall we do (Luke 3:10–14]?" He answered them: "He who has two coats, let him share with him who has none; and she who has food, let her do likewise." John's advice concerns what we do with our possessions and income and how they are obtained. Our vocation, our choice of employment, can itself be destructive to the Earth.

We do not exist in an isolated moment of time. Life is an unending stream. The delicate balances and rhythms and the intricate interrelationships built into the flow of renewal are wonderful to comprehend. We function in a web of life as seen in the web of a spider. Snap one strand and the entire web will collapse, for it is dependent for its wholeness on every single strand.

Gerard Manly Hopkins wrote: "Nature is never spent; / There lives the dearest freshness deep down things," and though it is not rational, it is majestic to see morning created "Because the Holy Ghost over the bent / World broods with warm breast and with ah! bright wings."[5] And Chief Seattle, the leader of the Suquamish tribe, when his people's ancestral lands were sold to the U.S. government in 1854, asked how one could sell the sky, the land, the freshness of the air, the sparkle of the water, our brothers the rivers, our sisters the flowers, the wind. For the Earth is our Mother and what happens to the Earth today, happens to us, her daughters and sons, tomorrow. He advised us to teach our children what his people taught their children: the Earth is our Mother. The Earth does not belong to humanity; humanity belongs to the Earth. All things are connected like the blood that unites one family. Whatever befalls the Earth befalls the sons and daughters of the Earth, for we did not weave the web of life; we are merely a strand in it. Whatever we do to the web, we do to ourselves.

Today the physical sciences are exploring and extending the realities of time and space, insisting that such things cannot be localized nor placed permanently. Scientists too are consciously awed by the new relationship between the elements of the universe and the oneness of earth as an organism. This new consciousness calls for metaphors for God that express God's participation and joy in Earth's complex processes and fecundity. As the scientist explores without—into outer space—the spiritual person seeks illumination within—into inner space. We are reminded that all the world is full of the glory of God!

In the prayer of Jesus in John 17:1–26, he asks God to make a holy people of believers, spared from the world's corruptions but not separated from them, that is, in the world but not of the world. Through these holy people Jesus asks God to sanctify the world through the Holy Spirit.

In Edward Robinson's *The Original Vision* one person recalls between the age of four and five walking on the moors, through the mist: "In that moment I knew that I had my own special place, as had all other things, animate and so-called inanimate, and that we were all part of this universal tissue which was both fragile yet immensely strong, and utterly good and beneficent. The vision has never left me. It is as clear today as fifty years ago, and with it the same intense feeling of love of the world and the certainty of ultimate good. . . . The whole of this experience has ever since formed a kind of reservoir of strength from an unseen force."[6]

"The earth is the Lord's and the fulness thereof."

Recently a piece of paper ignited our neighborhood to flames of passion. It was the last straw! There were more than enough shopping centers, restaurants, and office buildings standing empty, stretching into the sky, blocking out the light from flowers, trees, grass, and not least of all, people, and their growth. The piece of paper was a letter saying that a builder had purchased a small lot in the quiet neighborhood and was intending to cut down the trees and cover the land with a speculation house whose dimensions would fill the contour of the entire lot and offend the spirit of those who dwell there. The neighbors said no! They would fight for the quality of life they wanted for their children. The developers decided they would fight as well and employed expensive attorneys. If they won, the neighbors knew that the cancer would spread.

It reminded me of John Nichols' words:

> If these mountains die,
> where will our imaginations wander?
> If the far mesas are leveled,
> what will sustain us in our quest to be larger than life?
> If the high valley is made mundane by self-seekers and
> careless users, where will we find another landscape
> so eager to nourish our love?

And if the long-time people of this wonderful country are
carelessly squandered by Progress, who will guide us
to a better world?[7]

If mountains die and trees and neighborhoods are destroyed, air
and water is polluted, if concrete blocks out light and life, and if
people are herded into cement boxes without yards, we will have
lost a part of ourselves and of our Earth. We will lose much that
brings us into the presence of our Creator and which provides
energy, renewal, and hope so necessary to our being and creating.
If neighborhoods rise up and fight, however, we can protect our
Mother. Did the developer or the neighborhood win? I am happy
to report that the developer's request was denied!

In the Genesis story of creation God tells us to "Take care of my
garden!" ("The Lord God took the human, whom he placed in the
Garden of Eden to till it and keep it [Gen. 2:15].") We were
created to be gardeners. Long before we came to this land, the
American Indians knew that the garden, the land, belonged to
God. Chief Seattle once said, "This Earth is precious to the
Creator and to harm the Earth is to heap contempt upon its
Creator."[8]

Awakened eyes and ears will help us to see and hear. Annie
Dillard's *Pilgrim at Tinker Creek* is subtitled "A Mystical Excursion
into the Natural World." She writes about seeing. As a child she
would hide pennies and draw large arrows leading to them from
both directions, enjoying the excitement of the finder's discovery of
this free gift from the universe. Now grown, she still chronicles in
beautiful prose the free surprises and unwrapped gifts from Mother
Earth. Dillard writes, "The world is fairly studded and strewn with
pennies cast broadside from a generous hand. What you see is what
you get."[9] A saying is attributed to Jesus in the *Gospel According to
Thomas:* "The Kingdom of the Father is spread upon the earth and
men and women do not see it."

A group called The Greens advocates our working with local
municipal governments. They call for charter revisions to make the
local government directly answerable to the local people, so that
the people own and have custody over the essential resources of
nature in their own regions. The people then could set limits to
the abuse of nature around them.

God entreats us to "take care of my garden." Today those words are both a command and a warning.

Water: Cleansing and Renewal

Isaiah prophesied, "With joy you will draw water / from the wells of salvation [12:3]." The psalmist with confidence says of God, "You give them drink from your river of delights. / For with you is the fountain of life [36:8–9, paraphrased]"; and John invites all with these words: "Come forward; you who are thirsty; accept the water of life, a free gift to all who desire it [Rev. 22:17, NEB]."

The Israelites wandered in the desert, complaining to Moses of their need for water, for without water human beings perish. We are born in water; we are composed of water. We know our need for water, especially as we pollute our streams and rivers and oceans. The South Africans, arbitrarily taken from their villages to make new homes in the desert sometimes ten to twenty miles from water, know even more desperately the necessity for water.

Yet we long for more than physical water. We are thirsty, parched for the water of which Jesus spoke to the Samaritan woman at the well, the water of eternal life. When our lives are dry in the spiritual deserts through which we walk, we cry out for water in the wilderness. We long to experience Jesus' presence in our lives through prayer. He is our water, the water without which we truly perish. In John's Gospel the metaphor of water suggests the Spirit's influence: a flow of thoughts and words and actions in accordance with God's will. In the fourth chapter Jesus encounters the Samaritan woman and speaks with her of that "living water," of which he was the bearer. Anthony de Mello tells the story this way:

> The woman put down her water jar and
> went off to the town. She said to the
> people, "Come and see the man who has
> told me everything I ever did. Could this be the Messiah?"

Oh for a teacher like the Samaritan woman!

She gave no answers. She only asked a question.
It must have been tempting to
give the answer because she got it from you directly
when you said, "I am the Messiah. I
who am talking to you."

Many more became disciples because of
what they heard from his [Jesus'] own lips. They
said to the woman, "It is no longer because
of what you said that we believe, for we
have heard him ourselves, and we know that
this is, indeed, the Savior of the world."

I have been content to learn about you at
second hand, Lord. From scriptures and
saints; from popes and preachers. I wish I
could say to all of them, "It is no longer
because of what you said that I believe, for I
have heard him myself."[10]

The story says to me that I too am no longer content to hear about Christ second hand. Through prayer "I have heard him myself." We are—all of us—that Samaritan woman, disadvantaged, in desperate need, thirsty for water for our dried up spirits, yet needing to be convinced of its availability.

God gifts the Earth with rain that waters the grain to become our physical bread. Water is a necessity for physical survival, and water is a spiritual necessity as well. We are protected by water in the womb, born out of water, to be reborn with the water of the Spirit in baptism. For the Christian Jesus is that life-giving water. The writers of sacred scripture use water as a symbol of the source of life. Water is for drinking, for baptism, for blessing. The pouring out of water makes the gardens grow and deserts bloom. Without living water we dry up. It is also symbolic of cleansing, a washing agent; starting over, a renewing power; and letting go of false ambitions and pursuits of power and possessions, a sustaining resource. Like Moses we are first drawn out of the water to be saved and then emersed, or baptized, in the water in the name of the One who is also our spiritual water.

Jesus' first sign was the changing of water into wine, the miracle at Cana. John used the symbolism of the water in the purification rites of the Jewish people to say that with Jesus things change. There is transformation. Jesus used water to heal the blind man. He told him to wash in the pool of Siloam. At the pool of Beth-zatha Jesus met a man, ill thirty-eight years, whom he healed. Elisha told the rich leper Naaman to do the simple, humble thing of dipping in the river Jordan to be cured. Jesus met the Samaritan woman at the well. Water has curative power.

In the sacrament of baptism water represents the cleansing agent of God's grace, which welcomes us into the life of the Spirit. In the Old Testament the prophet Ezekiel said, "I will sprinkle clean water upon you, and you shall be clean [Ezek. 36:25]." Jesus himself was baptized by John in the Jordan river. The act of baptism was Jesus' moment of decision, response, and recognition. It marked the turning point in his life. When his work was finished, Jesus sent his disciples into the world to baptize in the name of the Father and of the Son and of the Holy Spirit.

Thomas Merton wrote about the wonder of water: "I am aware that the Easter Vigil retains many vestiges of primitive nature rites, and I am glad of it. I think this is perfectly proper and Christian. The mystery of fire, the mystery of water . . . made sacred and explicit by the Resurrection, which finds in them symbols that point to itself. The old creation is made solely for the new creation."[11]

Fire: Light of the Spirit

And God said, 'Let there be light,' and there was light.
—Genesis 1:3

The musician Leonard Bernstein once said that God never said "Let there be light," he sang it in the first four notes of Beethoven's Ninth Symphony, and every time God makes one of us, God sings again, "Let there be light." The psalmist sang, "The Lord is my light and my salvation [Ps. 27:1]," and Jesus said, "I am the light of the world. Whoever follows me will never walk in darkness, but will have the light of life [John 8:12]." Light is a symbol for the messianic age, and it is a symbol of "the way." Light allows us to see where we are and where we are going. There is a Hasidic story that goes like this: A young rabbi complained to the rabbi of Rizhyn: "During the hours when I devote myself to my studies I feel life and light, but the moment I stop studying it is all gone. What shall I do?" The rabbi of Rizhyn replied: "That is just as when a man walks through the woods on a dark night, and for a time another joins him, lantern in hand, but at the crossroads they part and the first must grope his way on alone. But if a man carries his own light with him he need not be afraid of any darkness."[12]

The inner light gives us our own light so that we need not be afraid of the dark. Some of us call it faith. Agnes Sanford's thesis in her book *The Healing Light* is that the whole world is full of the creative energy of God but that only the amount of it that flows through our own beings will work for us.

If we turn on an electric light and it fails to shine, we do not say, "There is no electricity!" but "There is something wrong with this lamp." Sanford writes, "We realize that while the whole world is full of that mysterious power we call electricity, only the amount that flows through the wiring of the iron will make the iron work for us. The same principle is true of the creative energy of God. The whole universe is full of it, but only the amount of it that flows through our own beings will work for us."[13]

Thomas Edison tried more than six thousand times to find a wire that could transmit a continuous flow of electricity, and at last he found what he needed. Edison believed he would succeed and used his imagination, the power of the mind to sense the possibility of things. Imagination creates and becomes real through belief. It is faith as the investment of energy that allows possibility to become reality.

Fire illuminates. It is the "light" of the spirit, the light within. When we experience God's light shining in our own darkness, we know the meaning of fire. Fire is emotion and energy, the release of energy from inert matter in the form of heat and light. We speak of people being "on fire" when we refer to them as emotionally charged.

The biblical writer expressed the importance of fire, imaging

God as a "consuming fire [Heb. 12:29]," the living flame of love; and it was in tongues of fire that the Holy Spirit came on Pentecost. Also, the psalmist wrote, "My heart became hot within me, and as I mused, the fire burned [Ps. 39:3]." And Matthew wrote that John the Baptist said, "'I baptize you with water, for repentance. But one who comes after me is mightier than I. I am not fit to take off his shoes. He will baptize you with the Holy Spirit and with fire [Matt. 3:11–12, NEB].'"

Sometimes when we want God's presence, because we believe God's peace will heal pain from which we are retreating, that pain may be the very flame of refining fire. Sometimes it is even possible that we enter the inner life to retreat from the external world; we have cultivated contempt for the sensual, material world of our bodies, our work, and our friends, contempt for nature and the world "out there." Meditation, however, is rooted in life, in wholeness of life.

Quietism can make a cult of sitting still, but contemplation is a gift of God. It is not a method nor a technique for feeling good. It is a way of being with God. It is emptiness filled with love for love's sake. For the spiritual life is a paradox. It includes dying and living, being lost and liberated in love. It means sitting still in order to serve and fire burning away the superficialities, the sterile preoccupation with possessions and illusions. Our goal is to live with the fire of passion for the presence of God. The tension between the dread and the desire survives the dark night of the soul, where the faint flame has flickered, until at last combustion occurs and unity is experienced. Where formerly life had been lived on the run, now one must sit in the middle of the fire, enduring its heat and pent-up, repressed passions, to teach the ego to listen to the spirit and to be touched and refined by it.

Music as Language of the Soul

Praise the LORD . . .
Praise him with the sounding of the trumpet,
praise him with the harp and lyre,
praise him with tambourine and dancing,
praise him with the strings and flute,

praise him with the clash of cymbals,
praise him with resounding cymbals.
Let everything that has breath praise the LORD. *Praise the* LORD.
—Psalm 150:1, 3–6; paraphrased

Music woos the muse of illumination. In C.S. Lewis's *Chronicles of Narnia* the Lion, Aslan, paced to and fro about the empty land, singing a new song. As he sang he called up the stars and the sun. And as he walked and sang the valley grew green with grass. It spread out from the Lion like a pool. It ran up the sides of the little hills like a wave. . . . Soon there were other things beside grass. . . . Trees! . . .In all directions it was swelling into humps . . . and from each hump there came out an animal. And Aslan continued to sing His creation into being.[14]

Those who care about creation say that we have lost our song and our story, that we need a cosmic story for today, a story of our unity, for the cosmos is in us and we are in the cosmos. With immediate communication possible around the planet, there grows a consciousness of the need for a cosmic spirituality. Yet throughout the history of Christianity there have been cosmic images to represent God. In 1125 Honorius of Autun wrote: "The supreme Artisan made the universe like a great zither upon which he placed strings to yield a variety of sounds."[15] The image of God as Musician creating the universe into one great zither, which harmonizes the cosmic music, is a cosmic story and a song for today.

Music is the language of the spirit, the language of prayer, for it can lift our spirit into the presence of God. With Bernstein we too hear God sing, for all creation is a song of praise to God. Through music we speak our longings and cry out our sorrows. In ancient Greece music was known as having healing powers, for music soothes the troubled soul. The biblical story tells us that the Spirit of the Lord departed from Saul and an evil spirit tormented him. Saul's attendants advised him to search for someone who could bring him music. When they brought David to Saul to play the harp, relief came to Saul, and the evil spirit left him (1 Samuel 16:14–23).

For the African, the drum with its beat, having been designed after the beat of the heart, is a communication between the creature and the Creator. Its beat is in time with the patterns of the universe. The drum, expressing the rhythms of nature, making possible communication in the spirit, is believed to be a healing instrument.

Music can bring us new life. I played a musical tape recording for a group of women I was leading on a spiritual retreat. When the music ended and we sat in silence, one of them whispered, "Now I can go home and face my problems with new strength." One by one they acknowledged, "I didn't think anything. I just felt alive."

Music helps us to pray. The Desert Fathers were fed by the songs of the psalms in the wilderness. The psalms were the bread by which they lived. In the harmony of music we too are fed, where heart speaks to heart in the wholeness of the language of music.

Music is the language of love. While caring for my six-month-old granddaughter, Lauren, who kept very late hours, I turned on the television in order to stay awake and saw the ending of the mythmaker Steven Spielberg's *Close Encounters of a Third Kind*. With awe I watched as the scientists of earth communicated with the people of a very advanced planet through the medium of music, the language of love, the language beyond words. I recalled how earlier that day Lauren and I had also communicated by singing strange but happy sounds, imitating one another.

Music heals and music communicates and music may even save. Mozart said that "Protestantism was all in the head," and the famous German Protestant theologian Karl Barth had a dream about Mozart. In his dream he was appointed to examine Mozart in theology. Because Barth had benefitted by listening to Mozart's music every day for years before going to work on his theology, he wanted to make the questions as easy as possible. He asked Mozart about his masses. But Mozart was silent. Thomas Merton was moved by Barth's account of his dream, because it concerned Barth's salvation. He suggested that Barth was admitting through his dream that he was saved more by the Mozart in himself than by his theology. It was the "divine child" in Mozart, his joy, spontaneity, and love that spoke to the scholar. But Merton comforted: "Fear not, Karl Barth! Trust in the divine mercy. . . . Christ remains a child in you. Your books (and mine) matter less than we might think! There is in us a Mozart who will be our salvation."[16]

Protestants are people of the head. Too often we have forgotten how to stand on our tiptoes in silence, holding our breath in wonder at the coming of the Lord. (And in preparation we think we had better be in proper order and decorum!) Yet when God comes, God slips in silently and sits huddled among the poor in spirit. When we become children again, recognizing the divine child in each of us and singing our praise to God with our hearts, and mouths, and bodies, we sing before God. A Sufi story says that Tansen was a great musician at the court of Akbar, and the emperor asked, "Who was your teacher?" Tansen replied, "He was a great musician, but more. I must call him 'music.' The emperor asked, "May I hear him sing?" and Tansen replied, "Yes, but he will not come to the court." So the emperor asked, "May I go to where he is?" "His pride may revolt, thinking that he is to sing before the king," Tansen explained. "Shall I go as your servant then?" asked the emperor and Tansen agreed, and the two went into the Himalayas, where the sage lived in his temple of music in a cave, in tune with the Infinite. The sage saw the emperor had come as a servant and sang when he was in the mood, and the singing was beautiful. It was a song of the universe. Akbar and Tansen went into a trance of rest and peace, and the master left the cave. He was gone when they opened their eyes. When they were home, the emperor asked the musician to sing for him and he did. "It is the same music, but it is not the same spirit. Why is this?" he asked, and Tansen replied, "The reason is this, while I sing before you, the emperor of this country, my master sings before God; that is the difference."

Unity of Body and Spirit

Do you not know that your body is a temple of the Holy Spirit within you, which you have from God?
—1 Corinthians 6:19

The harmonious chord that sounded upon the great zither of the universe is sounded by spirit *and* body. The body is not absent from spirituality. Living spiritually calls forth our total response, and the spirit and the body are a unity. It is not possible to value the spirit and devalue the body. Health demands wholeness. To cut off any part of ourselves, consciousness or unconsciousness, intellect or intuition, spirit or body or to withdraw from the world of sensation or the world of the spirit is to lose connection with reality. The surface of the skin is covered with trillions of biochemical reactions called sensations. An awareness of these is able to quiet the mind.

One of the biggest enemies to prayer is nervous tension. You relax when you come to your senses, such as breathe, hear, touch, and taste. Once, when emotionally agitated, I grabbed the cold frame of a lamp, and immediately the touch of cold returned me to my senses. We can move from thinking or talking, into the area of feeling, sensing, intuiting, and loving, where prayer can transform. Sensibility dies from too much living in the head.

Spiritual confusion is incompatible with bodily health, just as impoverished Earth can no longer feed the spirit. To be whole, we come to the feast of Creation, the banquet of life, with all the other creatures. Creation spirituality is a part of prophetic spirituality, a spirituality of spirit and body, of responsibility for oneself and for one's neighbor. Nachman of Bratslav once said that all the world and everything in it is a narrow bridge and that our task is to walk over it and not be afraid. Our task today is to bring the body of the cosmos and our own body back into balance and harmony. The body has a wisdom that we can trust. Because we are both body and spirit, we are able to see spirit in matter and matter in spirit. To reject the body is to reject the incarnation.

With the Age of Enlightenment a split between the body and spirit occurred. In the past ten years, however, an explosion of research has uncovered the effect that the mind has on the body and the body on the mind. Emotional states can translate into altered responses in the immune system. Loneliness and sadness do effect illness. Bernie S. Siegel's *Love, Medicine & Miracles* is his record of lessons learned about self-healing from his experience with exceptional patients, patients with hope and love. The book was on the *New York Times* best-seller list for more than a year. At Boston's New England Deaconess Hospital, Dr. Herbert Benson teaches persons with stress-related disorders to close their eyes and concentrate on a word or phrase for ten to twenty minutes. One study, as reported in *Newsweek*, November 7, 1988, found that although the clinic's hypertension program recognizes the need for medication, 80 percent of the patients were able to reduce their own blood pressure without it.

The Christian does not believe in a dualism of body and soul. The body is not an evil from which one flees but rather the temple of the living Lord over which and through which we celebrate. The body is the dwelling place of the spirit. The soul is incarnate. It is time for the forsaken body, which is starved or gorged, denied or overindulged, to be claimed, cherished, and inhabited. To lovingly listen to the body and its feelings—to find life in the body, in the integration of the body, soul, spirit, and intelligence through dream work, physical exercise, writing, and meditating—is to take care of oneself in order to take care of others.

In 1985, thousands of people celebrated the fiftieth anniversary of one of the most successful worldwide organizations in existence, Alcoholics Anonymous. The original and successful Twelve Steps for alcoholics have been modified to fit a number of other groups as well. But Alcoholics Anonymous recognizes the need for healthy intimacy and offers through the Twelve Steps a simple program of living in a process of recovery. Through the Twelve Steps we listen to the body and integrate it with the mind and spirit.

The person who integrates, who thinks with the heart, becomes the vessel of the Spirit and yet maintains that barefoot connection with Earth. The body has a wisdom of its own, an awareness of what is happening internally and externally. Metaphorically we nurture the rose, our self, through the winds and rains of adversity, pain, and suffering. We must be ready to win or lose, to sacrifice the ego's desires, to become free, unpossessed and unpossessing. Gradually, psychologically and, in some way, physically we learn to sing and dance and play in harmony with the cosmos. This is the joy of being in relationship with God, eating and drinking at God's banquet.

As the body becomes more aware, or as we become more conscious of the body's awareness, its messages appear clearer. Recently in a stressful situation, when a direct approach would have increased my stress, my body said "walk." After a great deal of walking and talking to myself, I found myself on a hill. I looked down on a city and suddenly was reminded of the story of Jesus looking down on Jerusalem and weeping: "Oh, Jerusalem, Jerusa-

lem, why . . ." I echoed his words and with that release I began to
sing. Knowing that Jesus had the same feelings of sorrow over the
ways we separate ourselves from one another reminded me of the
hope I have in Jesus. The gospel reminds us that we are neither
helpless nor hopeless, that there is new creation in Christ.

On another occasion, after an embarrassing episode, whenever I
recalled the event my body tensed. This happened for an entire
year. Alienation from ourselves blocks energy, which becomes pent
up in the body. To get in touch with our feelings of anger and fear
releases feelings of love and relaxation. And getting in touch with
our feelings eliminates the need for seeking acceptance from
others. To experience the adequacy of our own inner authority, to
love our self with the heart, requires listening to the heart and
body and accepting the feelings expressed. The kingdom of God is
to a great degree the harmony within that is projected and
expressed without, onto the world. And so we pray, "Renew my
spirit, refresh my soul, reenergize my body, ignite my mind that I
may be whole in You." We care for the body by providing an
ambience that encourages silence, such as soft music, to relax
tired, tense muscles, and that allows us to enjoy the present.
Caring for the body brings us closer to God.

Touch

Jesus spent a great deal of time healing bodies through the power
of his touch. Touch is a physical sign of love. Studies have shown
that infants will die without touch, so when Jesus blessed the
children, he touched them.

When Rilke wrote of love, he wrote of touch: "The love . . .
consists in this, that two solitudes protect and touch and greet
each other."[17] Older people and people who live alone often are
not touched enough. The church offers opportunities for such
people in the ritual of passing the peace in the worship service and
in welcoming the care of children in the congregation.

Movement

As the day awakens with the dawn stretching, we move our
bodies from the bed into the motions of daily life. For some, life is
a dance. When David brought the ark of God to Jerusalem, he
danced before the Lord with all his might (2 Samuel 6:1–15). The

movement of the dance gave expression, gave form to his feelings. David's dance represented his sense of the sacrament of life lived with God. In God's presence we yearn for the touch of the transcendent. When we dance with God we express our joy over being in God's presence.

We stand in awe at the wonder of our universe and of our unity in all creation. The immensity of God is all about us, within us, around us, and between us. Science has opened our minds. Now religion must open our eyes with wonder and awe to the beauty and unity of creation and our ears to the mystery and majesty of myth. Truth must dress in parable's colorful costume, and we must celebrate with our wholeness.

God fills our cup with ritual, story, music, and prayer, with the mercies and delights of God. Gertrud Mueller Nelson begins her *To Dance with God* by telling the story of her three-year-old daughter collecting long, bright strips of discarded cloth from her mother's sewing basket. When her mother checked on her, she found the child in the backyard sitting in the grass taping the scraps to the top of a long pole. "I'm making a banner for a procession," she said. "I need a procession so that God will come down and dance with us."[18]

When we are filled with joy over God's creation, we long to dance with God and wonder who placed that longing in our hearts. Some of us can no longer dance or are afraid to dance. When the ordinary becomes extraordinary, the secular sacred, the bread divine, then we can dance in our imagination, if not with our feet.

Bach asserted that although he played the notes, God made the music. And God continues to create the concert to which we may dance. Standing with awe at the wonder of our universe and of our unity in all creation, our spiritual being is continuously nourished as our ears stretch to hear the music of the spheres.

Knowing that men and women can only stand so much rationality and reason, Carl Jung tried to teach us to dance rather than to intellectualize our faith and rationalize our rituals. In dance before the Lord we express serious merriment, moving through the dichotomy of neither despising the world nor being consumed by our appetite for it. Movement of body, voice, or mind is the expression of the exuberance of our emotions. Without their expression we sometimes feel as if we will explode. Experiencing the sense of God's presence is like being showered by exploding fireworks in a summer sky. This is the kind of explosion Miriam expressed in her dance of joy over her people's victory, their freedom from bondage in Egypt (Exodus 15:20). Whenever we sense such freedom, our body asks to move. There is delight and joy in the movement of love: "When each partner loves so completely that he has forgotten to ask himself whether or not he is loved in return; when he only knows that he loves and is moving to its music—then, and then only, are two people able to dance perfectly in tune to the same rhythm."[19]

> Listen! My lover!
>   Look! Here he comes,
> leaping across the mountain,
>   bounding over the hills.
> —Song of Solomon 2:8, paraphrased

> I was daily his delight
>   rejoicing before him always,
>   rejoicing in his inhabited world
>   and delighting in humankind.
> —Proverbs 8:30–31

When King David danced before the Lord, his wife was shocked at his irreverence and told him so. The story says that she was barren the rest of her life. Without dance and song and prayer before God, we are barren.

In *The Greater Trumps* only Sybil could see the dance of the Fool, the Tarot card figure, and they asked her where. "There—no, there, no—it's moving so quickly I can hardly see it—there, ah it's gone away. Surely that's it, dancing with the rest; it seems as if it were always arranging itself in some place which was empty for it."[20] Sybil saw the Fool dancing everywhere, and in that dance she saw the sacred secret at the heart of the universe: the laughter and love of God. Dance makes manifest the invisible in sound and gesture and motion. Sybil saw the figure dancing everywhere, for the Fool was the incarnation of God.

Such movement need not always or ever be physical. To dance

before the Lord, to hear sweet music in prayer, is to approach the Earth as "Thou" rather than "It," pressing it to our hearts and releasing it, as a parent does the child. A sense of wonder, a dance of the spirit, a celebration of creation—experiences that once eluded us—become descriptions of new life we receive gratefully and knowingly.

Citizens of the Universe

Teilhard de Chardin, a citizen of the universe, believed the universe had bodily shape and soul. His was a vision of the universe in the process of self-creation. A twentieth-century Catholic priest and paleontologist, he saw matter and spirit as one. The law of the universe in his vision was a continually progressing spiritualization of the Earth and humanity. As an ordained priest Teilhard's salvation lay not in abandoning the world but in the Earth's fruition. As a qualified scientist his goal was that of releasing the Spirit from the ore in which it lay.

Teilhard de Chardin's spiritual life was completely dominated by a profound feeling for the organic realness of the world. That feeling of wonderment he could no more change than he could change his age or the color of his eyes. He saw with clear vision that the day was not far distant when humanity would realize that biologically it was faced with a choice between suicide and adoration. Yet his faith in God and in the world increased. Steeped in the divine presence, his was a reasoned optimism, the fruit of a deep interior life out of which he challenged us: "We must dare all things." Teilhard de Chardin hoped in the "cosmic" Christ, who "fills all in all [Eph. 1:23]."

All temporal things are paired into opposites. Yet there is a level of consciousness that transcends all categories or forms, that transcends all pairs and integrates them in wholeness and harmony in All, God. That which transcends all names, notions, or masks for the Unknown is expressed in silence through meditation; in sound through story and music; in action through touch, advocacy, and movement; in the senses through worship and service.

As creatures of the Earth we recognize our oneness in the unity of creation. The goal of the mystic is union with God in love, but one does not have to be a mystic to appreciate the wonder and riches of Mother Earth: food for the body, beauty for the eyes, nourishment for the spirit, harmony of silence and sound—from the first to the last a single whole. We live in a web of unity. Everything is connected to everything else. We pray for daily bread, and the bread we eat daily reminds us of God's love and presence, as do the rain and wind and clouds, for they too are all a part of us. When we eat the bread, we are eating months of sunshine and rain and snow. The psalmist tells us to *taste* and see that the Lord is good.

For many, the beauty and wonder of nature has convinced them of the love and oneness of the All. Brother Lawrence entered the Carmelite order as a lay brother when he was between fifty and sixty years old. At eighteen he had seen a tree stripped of its leaves and, aware that within a short time it would again be renewed with leaves and flower and fruit, he experienced a great love for God that increased as he aged.

Another story tells of students who were jealous of a fellow student, for it seemed to them that their master loved him, Ali, the best. Seeing their problem, the master gave them a test. Presenting each student with a small bird, he told them to take the birds to a place where no one could see them; there they were to kill them. At the end of the day the students returned with their dead birds and told of the difficulty they had in finding a place where no one would see them. Then the master turned to Ali and asked him about his bird. "I have returned my bird to its cage," Ali replied. The master asked him to explain. "You told us to kill the bird in a place where no one would see us, but I could not kill the bird, for everywhere I went, there was God."

Each of us has a piece of creation and all of creation is connected in one God. In knowing this we live in Reality, nourished at the banquet table of God's creation.

Chapter 6

Prophetic Spirituality

We pray to be fed; and because we are fed, therefore we feed. In worship we are fed. The ritual of coming together in the Spirit of the One who raised Jesus from the dead strengthens and nourishes us, so that when we get up off our knees, we go out into the world. In worship we take the bread, the bread of the word and sacrament. Jesus said, "Take, eat; this is my body . . . given for you." Bread represents Christ's body as we participate in the ritual of the sacrament of communion.

A ritual is a dramatic representation of a powerful and memorable experience. In the ritual the priest presents to us, as God's representative, the bread of God, the eucharist communion. Eating the bread together, drinking the wine, anointing worshipers, laying on hands are ritual, the tie that binds. Sacraments bathe us in divinity. Liturgy enfleshes the rational text and rescues meaning by dramatizing and reenacting the story. Liturgy liberates us from isolation.

The sacrament of Holy Communion is rooted in a sacred story: Once upon a time on the night in which Jesus was betrayed . . . We hear the story again and again, as it is reenacted in the ritual of communion and its power released. The real teacher is experience, and the story as experienced in the ritual transmits living energy and existential meaning.

"What is a rite?" asked the little prince. "They are what make one day different from other days, one hour from other hours," said the fox.[1]

I think that most of the time we take ourselves too somberly. Jesus certainly took life seriously. We have witness to that. The cross is no laughing matter. Yet on what basis or from what evidence, did Jesus' enemies gather their rumors of him as a wine bibber and a glutton? Jesus was serious but not somber.

Through the centuries pious preachers, playful and not so playful, have expounded on what Jesus meant by "unless you become as little children you will not enter the realm of God." Having worked and played with children most of my life, I may venture a playful perspective. (One more try will not tilt the universe.) Jesus meant for us to play, to pretend, to use our imaginations as children use theirs, for children are the most imaginative of us all. I believe in the sacrament of play. "Let's pretend" is participating in life 100 percent. Noticing a child at play, we witness a person 100 percent involved. All of us have experienced doing something we love or being with someone we love and having time stand still. We are beyond time. Perhaps this is what it means to experience eternity.

When Jesus broke the bread and gave it to his disciples, he said, "Take, eat, this is my body." When Sarah poured air into my cup and gave it to me, she said, "Take, drink, this is tea." Jesus said, "I am the door . . . the light . . . the sheepgate." Charles said, "I am a lion . . . a robot . . . a daddy." Children pretend and, for that moment, they are what they pretend.

In the eucharist we sit down with Jesus in spirit and in body, and we celebrate and rejoice in eating. In the story of Jesus' last supper, we hear that the disciples went out from the meal singing a hymn. Although I experience somberness in most eucharistic services, somehow in Jesus' eating and thanking and singing I note a lack of that quality. It *was* a serious moment. Jesus was on the way to the garden and betrayal, and yet they sang. We who take bread and eat together on the other side of the resurrection can do no less, for we are celebrating new life together. We are eating to fill our emptiness. And that takes special food, for we are hollow men and women seeking to become holy and healed (or at the least less lonely together). In "let's pretend" we use the holiest gift of all, the imagination. In hearing the story and eating together, we are in these moments of communion again children at the knees of Christ, playing, laughing, loving, going out singing, forgiven and healed.

Francis MacNutt in *Healing* gives Father John B. Healey's words concerning the sacramental act of healing through the eucharist: "Unquestionably the highlight of each day was the Eucharistic Liturgy celebrated in the evening. . . . In the final Eucharistic Liturgy a number of priests presented their physical ailments to Christ for healing through the ministering hands of brother-priests. In my own case, I was healed of a severe difficulty in swallowing food which was due to a hiatal hernia in the esophagus, and which caused me to regurgitate a portion of every meal I have taken in the last few years. This difficulty disappeared immediately after the Mass. It has not returned."[2]

We come to the communion table and eat the body, be it dry wafers or pieces from a loaf of bread, and drink the blood, be it wine or juice (and it does make a difference for some). For that moment we are with Jesus among our brothers and sisters. We pretend, and it does make a difference for that moment. For in that moment that we are eating with Jesus, we are forgiven and we are healed—and that makes all the difference.

A friend of mine at seminary recently participated in serving her first sacrament of Holy Communion (note the somberness of that sentence!). Suddenly she found herself without any bread. She had given it all away. There was no more. For the rest of the meal, the senior pastor while distributing the wine said to each taker, "Pretend to eat. It will count." Children would know what he meant. I think Jesus would too.

Having grown up in the church, I have taken the eucharist as a serious business. It is still that, but I need to remind myself again and again that it is also a playful event, for receiving forgiveness and new life is indeed an occasion for celebration. Eating together is a joyous moment. We are somber because the biblical story reminds us that the meal was Jesus' last supper, but Jesus returned to his friends after his resurrection. He stood on the shore, inviting them to breakfast, to fish and bread. In my imagination I can smell the fish frying on the shore, for Jesus is as present for me in the eating of fish and bread and wine with close friends as he is in the blessed bread and wine.

In guided imagery we can be in the presence of Jesus and return to Jesus whenever we need or want to. For the lover of God longs for God as a lover longs for the beloved, and God loves and longs for us. In the presence of the beloved there is fullness and

fulfillment, even when the loved one does nothing, but simply is.
The actual presence of the loved one, however, is so much more
fulfilling. It is as a miracle, undefinable and indescribable. So too
are the few times, now and then and far apart, in the midst of
much silence and absence, when we glimpse God or feel as if God
is present with us in the moment, through God's grace. It is
enough.

As we reenact the ritual of Holy Communion, we remember
Jesus' story, and we think of our own stories and those of others as
they interact with that story.

A girl had recently been confirmed into the membership of her
church. In her confirmation class she had been told the meaning
of the sacrament of Holy Communion, the eucharist, one of the
sacred mysteries. She had learned that some churches take the
grape juice, or wine, and the bread as the blood and body of
Christ. Other denominations celebrate in memory of Jesus' last
supper with his disciples in the upper room. All recall when "Jesus
took bread, gave thanks and broke it, and gave it to his disciples,
saying, 'Take and eat; this is my body.' Then he took the cup, gave
thanks and offered it to them, saying, 'Drink from it, all of you.
This is my blood of the covenant, which is poured out for many for
the foregiveness of sins [Matt. 26:26–28, paraphrased].'"

This was to be her first communion since she had become a
member of the church. She was excited and nervous as she walked
to the front of the church, kneeled, held out her hand, and
received the bread. Then the cup appeared before her, held in the
hands of the minister who a few days before had placed his hands
on her head as he prayed for her discipleship. He put the cup to
her lips to sip and to her surprise it slipped, spilling the wine on
her. Jesus' blood? It was a Holy Communion she would never
forget.

The small cups had been carefully filled with grape juice for the
chapel community's celebration of the eucharist. After the student
pastor had administered the bread and juice, someone returned the
small empty cups to the slots in the trays, piling each tray on top
of the others. The pastor was unaware that the trays were in a
precarious position, not equally filled. Suddenly he saw cups rolling

across the floor as quarters strewn from a slot machine. It was a Holy Communion he would never forget.

They walked to the front of the church, kneeling, praying, and offering their hands for the taking of the bread and wine. Their hands were open but empty. Instead of distributing the elements the minister asked them to choose either to "wash their hands of the whole thing," as Pilate had done, or to wash the feet of others in service and love, as Jesus had done. And when they were finished the altar was stripped and the black cloth of Good Friday placed upon it. It was a Holy Communion they would never forget.

One Good Friday I participated in the Greek Orthodox worship service. Father Alex, in showing me the new stained glass windows in his church, pointed to the pictures, explaining their sequence. "These are the sacraments," he said, "although we call them 'mysteries'." The service began at 7:00 p.m. with the chanting of the scriptures. People arrived in the narthex, bought a candle, kissed the icon, and offered their prayers. As I waited there for thirty minutes for a friend, it was obvious that this congregation was a family. There were smiles (for me as well) and hugs and kisses. The people showed their affection and spoke it aloud. By 8:00 p.m. two choirs had arrived, an adult choir and a children's choir, and the large sanctuary was crowded with worshipers. The service was sung in both English and Greek. When it was time for the congregation to participate in singing the Good Friday Lamentations, we all stood and sang from a printed booklet, one verse in English and the next in Greek, spelled out phonetically. We sang them back and forth. There was no organ or other musical instrument, but I have never heard more beautiful music. The children led us in the singing of the first station of the cross, and although we were singing a dirge, there was a sense of joy and love and of celebration in the presence of God.

It was truly a mystery, but it was an experienced mystery. As I sat there worshiping, I was reminded of the story the Greek author Nikos Kazantzakis told about gathering with the other faithful worshipers each Easter morning before sunrise at the tomb to see Christ arise. Every Easter they celebrated Christ's resurrection; that year the great theologian came from the city and preached to them

. . . and preached to them . . . and preached to them. That Easter the stone was not removed and Christ did not arise. We preach the story in order to experience Christ's presence in the story.

By 9:30 P.M. I was ready to go home. My Protestant one-hour worship habit is strong, but the most dramatic episode of all suddenly exploded before me. The sepulchre, banked in red and white flowers, was lifted on poles by six men and carried outside and around the great church. Each of us was given a lighted candle and followed. In the dark the candles glowed, and the singing filled the dark spaces. The Mystery lived among us. We returned to the sanctuary where one by one, beginning with the first rows, we went to the front of the church to kiss the cross, receive a flower, and be blessed by the priest. Because the priest was a friend, he kissed me on the cheek, welcoming me, a stranger to his tradition; and for me the foreign experience of kissing the cross was filled with unity, fellowship, and love.

The mystery of Holy Communion is to be experienced and remembered, as is the mystery of the death and resurrection of the One who initiated the sacrament. The sacrament of the eucharist is that in which participants are united to each other and to God.

Another memory of communion comes alive for me. One Sunday morning I had decided to remain in the pew rather than take communion, for I felt unworthy to participate in the eucharist. Suddenly I noticed that the minister, a visiting preacher from Scotland, was telling a story. He told of the lass who refused communion and of the pastor who cried out to her, "But, lassie, it was meant for thee." Jesus said, "Take, eat." Being human is being hungry, hungry for the bread Jesus supplies. The mystery of holy communion is beyond understanding. "It is meant for thee," whoever you are.

I am reminded of another time I took communion together with friends in the small chapel. There were so few of us that we gathered in the altar area where we could look into the faces of our sisters and brothers in Christ. Afterward a friend remarked, "As I looked at each person, I thought of how I loved them, of how much more God loves them, and of the words of the prophet: 'For you who fear my name the sun of righteousness shall rise, with healing in its wings [Mal. 4:2].'" And that reminded me of the summer I had spent a week at Padre Island in Texas with the family I love to which I have referred earlier. Sarah was three and Charles was five. I awakened early; when I saw the magnificent ball of brilliant red rising up out of the ocean, I called to Charles. A sleepy boy came into the living room, rubbing his eyes. He took one look at the sun and ran back to his bedroom. Bewildered, I asked, "What is the matter?" Immediately Charles emerged from his room, pulling his shirt over his head and shouting, "I had to dress for the sun." Now whenever I attend Wednesday's chapel service of Holy Communion at the seminary, I remember his words, and dress for the Son.

The celebration of a type of communion was caught in the film version of Isak Dinesen's lovely story "Babbette's Feast." A party of twelve bickering, foolish old Lutherans in Denmark, through the bread and wine, forgave and fellowshipped with one another because of Babbette's sacrifice and love for them. Having won 10,000 francs in the French lottery, Babbette (a political exile from France where she had been a gourmet cook) purchased, prepared, and served her friends a magnificent meal served in grand style. She spent the lottery money on this one feast. Toward the end of the film, a foreign colonel who attended told one of the spinster women, whom he had loved in his youth and with whom Babbette lived, how she had been in his thoughts all through the long years. "I will sit down with you every meal," he promised, "not in body, but in spirit."

Blessings

We sit down with Jesus at his table to be blessed. To bless is to focus with love on the other. To put a part of yourself into something to make it holy is to lean forward with love, to be there for the other. To bless and be blessed is to see the beauty and oneness of all of creation. God is always blessing, whether we recognize the blessing or receive it, whether we are open or closed to God's blessings.

It is only the divine blessing that enables us to bless. A good woman asked God to grant her one wish: that she would like to do good without knowing it. The wish was granted. Then with great wisdom God thought that the wish was such a good idea he would grant it to all persons. And so God did. Jesus blessed us and taught us how to bless and how to receive blessings. And Paul said, "I am content." Blessed is the person whose wants coincide with her needs.

Recently my "fake" grandchild, Sarah, had a birthday. When her mother asked Sarah what she would like for her birthday, Sarah was silent. She thought and thought, and then she said, "You, Mommy. I have the best gift already." Her mother was silent, as well, for Sarah was still thinking. "I think, Mommy, my best gift was being born."

Christianity is a religion of love and blessing. And from that abundance of love comes the doing of good. The Christian faith affirms that we are loved by God and that in that grace we are liberated and energized.

Tilda Norberg and Robert Webber have written of the power of prayer and of the sacraments in healing in *Stretch Out Your Hand*.³ They give examples of healing; answer frequently asked questions about healing; and suggest ways of praying for oneself, for another's healing, and for the social order. They offer ways in which healing can become a more important part of the church community. In the chapter "Praying for the Social Order," they relate prayer and worship to work and prophetic spirituality, exploring the distinctively spiritual resources of the Christian faith for healing the brokenness of social institutions.

There is a need for social healing. One need only turn on the television, read the newspaper, sit in the sanctuary or at our family table to know so. Wherever we work or worship, vote or volunteer, we are aware of separation and injustice and of the need to "feed."

Jesus announced his ministry with the words from Isaiah, "The Spirit of the Lord is upon me, because he has anointed me to preach good news to the poor. He has sent me to proclaim release to the captives and recovering of sight to the blind, to set at liberty those who are oppressed, to proclaim the acceptable year of the Lord [Luke 4:18]." We are asked to do likewise.

In *Jesus Means Freedom*, Ernst Kasemann tells about a strict parish bound to God's commandments, bound to keep the Sabbath holy. In 1952 Holland was experiencing severe storms and floods. On one particular Sunday if the parish inhabitants were to survive the dyke had to be strengthened. The pastor was, therefore, in great religious difficulty: Should he call out the people of the parish to work, even if this would profane the Sabbath, or should he abandon them to destruction and honor the Sabbath? The personal decision was too much for him to make alone, so he summoned his church council. They decided that we live to carry out God's command and that God, being omnipotent, can always perform a miracle with the wind and waves. Their duty they saw as obedience in life or death! The pastor, concerned for his flock, tried one last argument, perhaps against his own conviction: Did not Jesus himself, on occasion, break the fourth commandment and declare that the Sabbath was made for human beings, not humans for the Sabbath? Thereupon a venerable old councilman stood up and said: "I have always been troubled, Pastor, by something that I have never yet ventured to say publicly. Now I must say it. I have always had the feeling that our Lord Jesus was just a bit of a liberal."[4]

Made in the image of God, all persons are our sisters and brothers. "Have we not all one Father?" the prophet asks, and Cain's question, "Am I my brother's keeper?" still haunts us. The phrase "made in the image of God" also gives us a promise of hope no matter how despairing the picture of human evil appears. To be human is to be wounded. We bear the wound and are aware of the wound that only Christ can heal. And when we are fed and our wounds are being healed, Jesus says, "Feed my sheep."

So go out we must, to heal and to feed, for the function of ritual is to send one out, not to wrap one up where one has been all the time.

Service of Work

> And what does the LORD require of you?
> To act justly and to love mercy
> and to walk humbly with your God.
> —Micah 6:8, paraphrased

The early church father Anselm in a sermon told an apocryphal story of Justice and Mercy, who were arguing as they looked down at the world in 1 b.c. Justice declared that the world must be destroyed. How else could justice be maintained? Mercy, however, replied, "Then where will I be?" At last, after much discussion and debate, the divine Logos solved their dilemma, saying, "Trust me. I will satisfy you both." When Christian spirituality was inaugurated at Pentecost with the coming of the Spirit, all persons were called to be prophets, initiators of mercy and justice.

There is a story of a woman who wanted to see heaven and hell. In hell she saw a banquet table heaped with delicious, gourmet food placed on fine china. The people wore rich clothes on thin bodies because they could not eat; and they gnashed their teeth, for though the table was spread, the only implements were three-foot-long forks. They could not maneuver the food into their mouths. When the woman was taken to heaven, she saw the same table, but here the people were plump and joyous, for though they had the same implements, they were using the three-foot-long forks to feed one another.

The spiritual hunger of the human heart cannot be separated from the physical hunger of the world. The right to have a share of earthly goods sufficient for oneself and one's family belongs to everyone. We ask for bread daily, but the bread for which we ask is "our" bread. When in our Lord's prayer we pray for our bread, God asks:

> Is not this the kind of fasting I have chosen:
> to loose the chains of injustice
>   and untie the cords of the yoke,
> to see the oppressed free
>   and break every yoke?
> Is it not to share your food with the hungry
>   and to provide the poor wanderer with shelter. . . ?
> Then shall your light break forth like
>   the dawn, . . .
>   —Isaiah 58:6–8, paraphrased

What will I do and who will I be when I get up from my knees and come out of my silence? Spirituality is for action. Prayer is our response to God and is love in action, as the sacred stories tell us over and over.

All of his life a monk had prayed for a visitation by Mother Mary. At the last moment the Mother arrived. The monk was in ecstasy. But in the midst of this mighty moment, the bell rang to feed the hungry. "Oh, Mother, I must leave. I am so sorry. Please stay." He offered Christ's food to the poor and returned to his cell, miserable with disappointment. To his surprise, however, Mary was still there. "You stayed!" he exclaimed. "Yes," she replied. "However, if you had stayed, I would have gone."

Sarah, Deborah, Abraham, Moses, Isaiah, and Jeremiah answered God's call to go. It is not easy to be a prophet. "Moses," God called, and before Moses' encounter with God was finished, he had made all kinds of excuses to avoid his prophetic calling.

The rabbi said, "There is a full-fed zaddik [saintly person]." His disciples asked him what he meant by this. "Well," he explained, "While a person may buy a loaf of bread and eat it, another buys and shares the bread with others." Spiritual fullness comes through sharing with others.

Humans can feed each other only for so long before they realize their need for more than bread or flesh. What community is there apart from God? We are asked, "Why do you work for bread that perishes [John 6:27, paraphrased]?" Life in the spirit, life in prayer, is to share our food. Once in my imagination I saw a gourmet cook who had traveled around the world, tasting and preparing magnificent meals and delicious desserts. I asked him, "What is the most beautiful meal you have ever eaten?" The gourmet cook was silent. He thought of all the fine, expensive, even royal foods he had tasted and prepared. "The most beautiful meal?" he questioned. "The most beautiful meal," I repeated. "The most beautiful meal I have ever eaten," said the gourmet, his eyes filling with tears, "was the crust of bread I shared with a hungry child."

The service of worship and work is not only prayers of praise and thanksgiving for the blessedness of life but pleas for mercy and justice. The Hebrews believed that the entire cosmos stood on two pillars. As the psalmist wrote: "Justice and righteousness are the pillars of your throne [89:14, paraphrased]."

Isaiah found God in the Temple; Elijah, in a still small voice; Moses, in a burning bush; Mother Theresa, in the hovels of India.

Some of us find God in the pulpit; and others, on the picketline. God is there, where are you?

Jesus as Prophet

Jesus said, "I have come that you might have abundant life." The Native American says, "Wisdom is 'that the people may live'."

In a world of need and want, where three quarters of the people go to bed hungry every night; where 5 percent of the population owns and uses 35 percent of the natural wealth; where the needlessly unemployed, the handicapped, abused, gay, Native American, refugee, black, child, woman, and minority have become victims; where seventeen billion dollars per year would provide adequate food, water, education, health, and housing for everyone in the world and where the world spends that amount on military arms every two weeks; where 18,000 jobs are lost for every billion dollars spent on military; where there is apartheid in South Africa and war in many countries—in this world it is time to speak and listen to prophetic voices from the past and present. It is time for justice, peace, liberation, healing, and hope.

Jesus ministered to the *anawim*, the forgotten and oppressed ones. Jesus revealed hope. When the rich man went away sorrowing because he could not give up his wealth, the people listening asked Jesus, "Who then can be saved?" Jesus replied, "What is impossible for human beings is possible with God." And Jesus replied that all things were possible for God.

Jesus was a prophet. "My food," said Jesus, "is to do the will of the one who sent me and to finish [the] work [John 4:34]." Jesus called for inner and outer conversion. His was a prophetic call to the community of humankind, a community oriented and committed to justice for all. Each of us is called to build up community through homemaking, maintaining the earth, singing, becoming a saint, or being a child. It is possible that each of us can become prophetic in our profession. Jesus as a prophet heals our blindness and transforms our vision of the world. He gives us not a title but a towel and says, "Whoever would be great among you must be your servant . . . even as the Son of man came not to be served but to serve [Matt. 20:26–28]." Christian spirituality calls us to relate to others with compassion and to care for their needs. Participating in God's banquet here and now with others is taking up the towel and forgetting the title.

It was just before the Passover Feast and Jesus knew that the time had come for him to leave this world and go to God. The evening meal was being served to Jesus and his disciples, and knowing that he had come from God and was returning to God, he got up from the meal and wrapped a towel around his waist, poured water into a basin, and began to wash his disciples' feet, drying them with the towel that was wrapped around him. When he was finished washing their feet, he asked if they understood what he had done and said to them that he had set them an example and they should wash one another's feet, for no servant is greater than the master (John 13:1–17).

The towel is a symbol of service to others. We may begin by seeking a title. "Let me be called your friend, your beloved, your child." But we are asked to serve.

The Old Testament prophets heard God's call to prophetic spirituality through their prayers, and they went out to meet the world, thus meeting God there as well. But to be a prophet is to take a very great risk. For when the angel comes to you, saying "Fear not," it is time to watch out.

Matthew Fox, an exponent for prophetic spirituality, has listed the signs of a true prophet as personal rerooting, reluctance, creativity, and community orientation. About reluctance he writes, "Another sign of the prophet in each of us is a certain reluctance, a shyness to accept the burdens of one's prophetic vocation."[5] We find reluctance in Moses, in Jeremiah, in Isaiah, in Mary, and certainly in Jonah. The reluctance comes from a desire for savoring life rather than for paying the price the prophet must pay. But the desire to share the savoring of what one has tasted is greater than the fear.

Works Versus Grace

On the south side of the great door of the cathedral in Basel, St. Martin is pictured on his horse. Originally he was feeding a beggar, but at the time of the Reformation the beggar was removed out of fear that people would think they could earn salvation through their works. *Sola gratia* is a fundamental tenet of the Christian faith. "For it is by grace you have been saved, through faith—and this not from yourselves, it is the gift of God—not by works, so that no one can boast [Eph. 2:8–9, paraphrased]." When we serve others we give up the right to be in charge, for it is God who gives. And Paul continues: "For we are God's workmanship, created in Christ Jesus to do good works, which God prepared in advance for us to do [v. 10, paraphrased]."

The question is not which is more important, grace or works, but what is the motive? A brother said to Abbot Pastor: If I give one of my brothers a little bread or something of the sort, the demons spoil everything, and it seems to me that I have acted only to please men. The elder said to him: Even if your good work was done to please, we must still give to our brothers what they need. And he told him this story. Two farmers lived in a village. One of them sowed his field and reaped only a small and wretched crop. The other neglected to sow anything at all, and so he reaped nothing. Which of the two will survive if there is a famine? The brother replied: The first one, even though his crop is small and wretched. The elder said to him: Let us also sow, even if our sowing is small and wretched, lest we die in the time of hunger.[6]

It is through God's grace that we can perform our service of work, sharing with others. Paul said that he could do all things "through Christ," and God's message through Christ is "Here I am, hanging on a cross, not hiding in a chapel or a cell." Life in the Spirit is love in action. So we pray in order to feed and feed in order to pray, for through prayer we become compassionate and love only because God first loves us.

Must these be dichotomies: works or grace? prayer or action? the temple or the street? We need not separate them. In the tension of opposites there is energy. Karl Barth once said, "Only the doer of the word is its real hearer." And thanks belongs to God.

"Who Will Go?"

All glory and thanks belong to God. It was in the temple that Isaiah saw that glory and heard the call, as we read in Isaiah 6:9.

Then flew one of the seraphim to me, having in his hand a burning coal which he had taken with tongs from the altar. And he touched my mouth, and said: "Behold, this has touched your lips; your guilt is taken away, and your sin forgiven." And I heard the voice of the Lord saying, "Whom shall I send, and who will go for us?" Then I said, "Here I am! Send me." And he said, "Go."

As a response to God's love, our worship arises from our inner self as an expression of thankfulness. Because our lips have been touched with the bread of life ("this is my body") and the wine of the cup ("this is my blood"), our hearts and our feet move. Rabbi Abraham Joshua Heschel, past-professor of mysticism and ethics at Jewish Theological Seminary in New York City, joined his prayer with his prophetic spirituality in his teachings, his writings, and his person. When he marched in the civil rights demonstration at Selma, Alabama, he called his action one of "praying with our feet."

"Who will go?" God asks, seeing the misery of the people. God asks, but does not coerce. God asks in the beauty of the temple, in the silence of the closet, in the bedroom on a sleepless night, "Whom shall I send, and who will go for us?" The words recall the story in chapter 2, "The Board Meeting": "Will you go, my beloved, will you go?" "Go" may mean leaving home to go far away as Abraham did, or entering into a slave camp, into the place of hard, cruel labor, as Moses did. "Go" may mean spending twenty-seven years in a South African prison or dying in a Nazi concentration camp. "Go" for Mother Teresa of Calcutta means to go into the streets among the homeless and the hungry, into the prison and places of women and men in bondage to addiction and dependency. "Go" may even mean simply returning home from the temple to our daily tasks with renewed vigor and vision. Go to your next meeting, class, appointment, chore with love. "Go," say the biblical storytellers, asking us to participate in the story; put on the feelings of the characters and identify with the story as our own story. Respond to it here and now.

Service of the Lord

In a class on Jewish spirituality, Dr. Ian Russ of the University of Judaism told the story of Rabbi Nahmann. Hearing a foolish prayer at the close of the Day of Atonement, the rabbi spoke to the one who prayed, saying, "I know that on the Eve of Atonement you prayed for one thousand rubles all at once so that business would not disturb you from prayer. On the morning, knowing that that much money would tempt you to begin a new business and have, therefore, even less time to pray, you asked for one half the amount every half-year. But before the gates closed, you changed your prayer to quarterly installments in order to learn and pray without being disturbed. But what makes you think your prayer is needed in heaven? Perhaps it is your toil that is needed instead." Prophetic spirituality is service of the Lord. It is God we serve in serving others.

"Where are you?" God asks, and Adam hides to escape his responsibility. The question is asked to awaken our awareness of our need to be honest and to face the consequences of our acts. Yet we want answers. We seek understanding. And what is the answer to where we are? One possible answer is this: praying. Another: prophesying. Others are fasting and eating. Observe what your heart and head and faith-journey with God tell you. What attracts you? This is your way. This is where you are.

When as Christians we read and hear the story of the Israelites in bondage in Egypt under the oppressor Pharaoh, we know instinctively that the oppression is wrong. "The Lord said, 'I have indeed seen the misery of my people in Egypt. I have heard them crying out because of their slave drivers and I am concerned about their suffering [Exod. 3:7, paraphrased].'" We know oppression is wrong because we believe that everyone is created in the image of God and no one should be a slave to another. Most of us have grown up believing in freedom and liberty for all, although we may not see it in action at all times. Those of us who have grown up in the Christian church are helped in various ways to be aware of evil and to fight for the underdog, the one who is powerless and bound. Many of the psalms speak of God's concern for the oppressed: "[God] will defend the afflicted among the people and save the children of the needy; God will crush the oppressor [Ps. 72:4, paraphrased]." And when the Israelites, released from their bond-age, in turn became the oppressor, the Lord spoke out against them. God is more concerned with justice than with privilege. "I hate, I despise your religious feasts; I cannot stand your assemblies [Amos 5:2, paraphrased]." "And what does the Lord require of you?" God's messenger, Micah asks. "To act justly and to love mercy and to walk humbly with your God [6:8, paraphrased]."

"Then I saw a new heaven and a new earth, for the first heaven and the first earth had passed away [Rev. 21:1, paraphrased]." "In keeping with his promise we are looking forward to a new heaven and a new earth, the home of righteousness, the place where justice will be at home [2 Peter 3:13, paraphrased]." Yet a new birth does not come without the pangs of labor, the terror of transformation, the cost of courage and sacrifice. The world cries out for transformation, for new thinking, new compassion, new creation. When Mahatma Gandhi was asked what he thought of Western civilization he replied, "I think it would be a good idea." Gandhi accepted the Christian's Christ but not their Christianity.

The church today is called upon again to become prophetic, to initiate the people into God's plan and purpose, to break and be broken for the sake of the New Creation, to use the chaos of creation for creativity, the anger of injustice for transformation, the energy and power of the Holy Spirit for self-expression. God's call is for compassion in one's work, for freedom from oppression, away from legitimizing the oppressor, so the word that goes out "from my mouth" does not "return to me empty [Isa. 55:11]."

A myriad of stories could be told to illustrate injustice. Allan Boesak, in *Black and Reformed,* tells the story of the twelve-year-old boy who was caught stealing fruit from a farmer's storeroom. The farmer tied him to a pole, whipped him, and left him there for the night. Seeing what had happened, a black evangelist untied the boy in the middle of the night and took him to his parents. The next day the farmer and his two sons caught the evangelist, tied him to a pole, and beat him to death with sticks and a hose pipe. When brought before the judge, each of them was fined $85.00.[7]

A friend of mine, a young white student, was traveling by plane to Durban, South Africa, and sat beside an elderly white gentle-man. "What is the population of Durban?" she asked. "Five hundred thousand," he answered. Surprised, she said, "I thought it was a bigger city." "Well, if you are going to count everyone," he replied, returning to his newspaper.

Jesus offered a new way of looking at God and our sisters and brothers when he came to help those in need: the outcasts, the lepers, the whores, the centurion.

Finding Self and Forgetting Self

In the service of work and love, we find ourselves. Psychologists tell us that we cannot give away what we do not have and, therefore, must discover and create a healthy ego before we can give it away. It is when we find ourselves in God that we can give ourselves away to a neighbor. Praying brings us into the presence of God who loves us, summons us, and then sends us into action and into forgetting ourselves.

Each person is unique in the world, a new thing, and each is called upon to fulfill her or his particularity. Whatever you do may be a way to me, says God, provided you do it in such a way that it leads to me.

In the class I mentioned previously, Dr. Russ also told the story about the Seer of Lublin who when challenged to "show me one general way to the service of God," replied, "It is important not to tell persons which way they should take. For one way to serve God is through learning, another through prayer, another through fasting, and still another through eating. Everyone should carefully observe which way his or her heart draws, and then choose this way with strength." The good rabbi was advising us to learn but not to imitate, for each of us is unique. We will perform a new service according to our character, teachings, and actions; and though each of us has access to God, each has a different access. The Seer continued, "What sort of God would it be who has only one way in which to be served! Whatever you do may be a way to God, provided you do it in such a manner that leads to God."

Living in the spirit is hallowing the world with one's whole being. One who is a unity of body and spirit is one whose work is all of a piece. When we have found ourselves in Christ, we can forget ourselves for others. The work we are destined to perform upon the world is not only for our own salvation, but also for the other's. This is finding and forgetting oneself. In that finding and forgetting we hear Jesus' words, "Feed my sheep!"

"Feed My Sheep!"

We have been fed at the banquet, and Christ is the bread. John's last story is the story of our commission to prophetic spirituality. In the last chapter of John's Gospel, Jesus discovered that his disciples had been fishing all night. Early in the morning Jesus called out to them, "Friends, have you any fish?" And he told them what to do. They obeyed and were unable to haul the net in because of the large number of fish, and then they recognized their Lord. "Come and have breakfast!" he called. Come to the banquet, the messianic banquet where "all will be well and all will be well and all manner of thing will be well."[8] When they had finished eating, Jesus said to Simon Peter, "Do you love me more than these?" Three times he asked Peter in order to move him from the broken relationship (brought about by his denial that he was one of Jesus' disciples) to a restored one. In the fourth Gospel, to love means to keep Jesus' commandments, even to laying down one's life for one's friends (15:13), so when Peter affirmed that he loved, Jesus replied, "Feed my sheep."

To feed is important. Food is less so, unless you have none. To feed or be fed is to hear God speak about us, what God wants us to do or to become. The words that God utters are different words to each of us: "Feed my lambs," "Be brave," "Be merciful," "Heal my creation," "Feed my sheep!" We choose how we will feed. We choose whom we will feed, and sometimes, with Peter, we are confused as to whether we have chosen well. Then come the words "Follow me!" How do we discern what we are meant to do, where we are to go, how we are to feed, and even what it is we will eat and from whom we will take our food?

Over and over when I have prayed for discernment and understanding, the words return, "I did not ask you to understand. I asked you to love." Recently, however, when I needed help in the direction I should take, I read Norberg's and Webber's[9] list of steps in the discernment process, and I put them into action. I experienced the direction that I was seeking. My experience since that time leads me to affirm again the power and purpose of prayer. The following are steps in praying for discernment:

1. Tell God how you feel as honestly as you can.
2. Invite God into all your brokenness, and ask God to heal you and show you what to pray for and what to do.
3. Sit in God's presence silently.
4. Pay attention to what happens in the silence, what images, thoughts, and memories arise.
5. Imagine Jesus with you.
6. Jot down impressions that come as you pray.
7. Look for a pattern that suggests a direction for prayer, and trust what comes.
8. When nothing happens, do not become discouraged. Keep asking, and remember that God speaks in a variety of ways.
9. Trust that the Holy Spirit will correct you if your discernment is inaccurate, and continue to remain as open as possible.
10. When discernment does not come immediately, continue to pray, "bearing God's beams of love."

We choose (or hear) the words that make meaning for our lives, sometimes even the words that tell us we must die for Jesus' sake in order to feed his lambs.

Listening and Hospitality: Mary and Martha

For many the story of Mary and Martha illustrates a conflict between spiritual matters and mundane matters, chores and commitments. Martha was fussing and fretting over the fact that Mary was sitting and "doing nothing," and Mary, sitting at Jesus' feet, was unaware of Martha's busyness (was it not good and holy business?). According to *The Cloud of Unknowing*, Mary gazed at Jesus with deep delight and all the love of her heart, "eagerly reaching out into that high cloud of unknowing that was between her and God." But what she was looking at was the supreme wisdom of Jesus' Godhead shrouded by the words of his humanity. The anonymous writer of *The Cloud of Unknowing* explains that in the cloud of unknowing Mary experienced the "many secret movements of her love," because this is the highest and holiest state of love known on earth. Mary was so deeply immersed she did not hear Martha's words of complaint, and this is the example our author meant for all actives and contemplatives. [10]

Yet Martha's complaining can be understood and excused under the circumstances. She spoke without knowledge. So it is true of complainers today about God's special servants, because the former have no idea of any kind of life better than their own!

Contemplatives must excuse and ignore what others say and do to them, the author continues, as Mary did. Then Jesus will do for them what he did for Mary, defend her who loved him. Jesus defends the contemplative. "Martha, Martha, you are worried and upset about many things, but only one thing is needed. Mary has chosen what is better, and it will not be taken away from her." Actives are busy, as Christian charity requires. What Martha was doing was good. Who can fault her caring for the physical needs of a loved one? But in order that she might not think that what she was doing was the highest and best, Jesus said that only one thing is needed: That God is loved and praised.

The first service of work is listening to others. Through experience and compassion we know the healing power of listening. We do not need the wisdom of giving the correct answer. The hospitality of listening is not to give answers, but to bear one another's burden. It is the ability to pay attention to the guest without preoccupation with one's own needs and worries, to break through the narrowness of fear and open one's home and heart to the guest. To pay attention one must be at home in his or her own house. The center of life, the energy of inspiration, and the deep source of guidance are in one's own heart.

Mary listened to Jesus. She sat at his feet, and he said, "Mary has chosen the better part." The story of Mary and Martha is a story of listening and hospitality, a story of paradox, the paradox of praying and prophetic spirituality, but the story is comfortable with paradox and ambiguity. True hospitality for Mary included the human-divine encounter, choosing to live in the now, in the spiritual awareness of Christ's presence, and forsaking the things that cluttered her life.

Growing up in the Protestant tradition where the work ethic was powerful, I learned early that sitting still was a disservice to God. I carried this false guilt for a long time. Recently I heard that there are only two real guilts, hurting another and separation from God. Knowing this has been beneficial to my prayer life. I now have permission to be with God doing nothing. Mary chose to *be* with Jesus. It was enough.

St. Bernard named three vocations in the monastic life: that of Lazarus, the penitent; Martha, the active servant of the monastic house; and Mary, the contemplative. He tried to solve the separation by saying that Mary and Martha as sisters should supplement one another and dwell together in peace. For Bernard, the contemplative life was the one the monk should prefer, though the active life was necessary. In the end, the best possible life is found in union.

We live today at a time when we search for and work for peace and justice; we ask why some people are without bread. Our world has become a global society, and we are called to work toward a new heaven and a new earth, a global civilization of justice and peace and ecological harmony. The outcast, the marginized, the *anawim*, the so-called helpless ones, remind us of humility and courage. They are we, and we are they, and we are one. Justice and injustice is in the bread I eat, the coffee I drink, the money I spend, the vote I cast. When I eat my bread and remember those who have no bread, God cries. God not only cries but judges such a world.

In a small book I received unsolicited, *Sometimes God Has a Kid's Face*, Father Bruce Ritter, the author, tells stories of America's exploited street kids with whom he has worked for more than twenty years. In that time more than one hundred thousand homeless kids have come in off the streets to find shelter and love at Covenant House. Degraded, hurt, lonely, hungry, and lost children ages nine through twenty-one have come to Father Ritter because they have nowhere else to go. One-third of them make it back into life, but the rest die young, go to jail, or join the drug inhabitants of the streets. He writes that covenant is an agreement between persons to commit themselves to each other with honor, respect, support, and love. This is the meaning of Covenant House. The people who live there are not there for God-talk, for most of them have never experienced love. When one of the young men, Rick, said "God *never* did anything for me," Father Ritter replied, "I think God sent you here." "No, he didn't," retorted

Rick. "I needed a place to stay. . . . Why should God care about what happens to me?"

"Did you ever fall in love with somebody? Really in love? . . . Did they ever ask you why you loved them? Did you have a reason?" asked the father. "No," Rick replied. "Neither does God. He doesn't need to have you love him back," said the father. "That's good," said Rick, "because I don't."

Father Ritter told this story in connection with being interviewed for a documentary filmed about street kids and Covenant House. After learning of Ritter's discomfort over being interviewed, Rick hugged the father and Father Ritter hugged him back. At the end of the interview, when the reporter asked the father, "Why do you do what you do?" Father Ritter replied, "I do what I do because of God. And sometimes God has a kid's face."[11]

Jesus said very clearly that mercy—feeding the hungry, clothing the naked, giving shelter to the homeless, comforting the lonely and the ill, loving the marginized—was the meaning of prayer, for prayer is compassion, not dogma nor doctrine.

Our response to evil, our covenant with the world and God, determines whether we are or are not, will or will not become, a prayerful person. Our Lord taught us how to pray by showing us how to love. Paul tells us that made in the image of God "we, with our unveiled faces reflecting like mirrors the brightness of the Lord, all grow brighter and brighter as we are turned into the image that we reflect; this the work of the Lord who is Spirit [2 Cor. 3:18, paraphrased]."

My granddaughter Lauren, when she was a year and a half, stayed with me while her parents were away. Because my surroundings were new, I put her crib beside my bed so I could be there for her if she awoke during the night. She did, as I expected, and cried. "It is all right, I am here." I repeated over and over, for there was nothing else I could do for her. My desire was that she trust me. In the daylight I realized that God as Parent assures me over and over, "It is all right. I am here." God's desire is that I trust. And the next afternoon when Lauren did not want to take a nap, I insisted, even through her tears, because I knew it was best for her. I am learning that God knows what is best for me, even through my tears and doubts, for God's call to prayer, to worship, and to service is Love calling to love to come to the banquet! God's power is the power of love. God's food is God's presence and love, and because God first loves us, we are enabled to love.

Through story and scripture, prayer and meditation, music and movement, dreams and journalizing, worship and service we are invited to come to the banquet. We come to the banquet to be fed so that we may return to the world to feed.

Notes

Chapter 1—Christian Spirituality

1. Anonymous, *The Cloud of Unknowing and Other Works*, trans. Clifton Wolters (New York: Viking Penguin, 1978), 100.
2. Julian of Norwich, *Showings* (New York: Paulist Press, 1978), 308.
3. Thomas Merton, *What Is Contemplation?* (Wheathampstead, Hertfordshire: Anthony Clarke, 1975), 89.
4. Julian, *Showings*, 296.
5. Theophane the Monk, *Tales of a Magic Monastery* (New York: Crossroad, 1981), 89.
6. Martin Buber, *Tales of the Hasidim Later Masters* (New York: Schocken, 1948), 241.
7. Julian, *Showings*, 267.
8. Ibid., 270, 271, 278.
9. *Cloud of Unknowing*, 183–84.
10. Benedicta Ward, *The Sayings of the Desert Fathers* (London: Mowbrays, 1975), 61.
11. Ibid., 6.
12. The author heard this story told by a storyteller.
13. Buber, *Later Masters*, 210.
14. Richard J. Foster, *Celebration of Discipline* (New York: Harper & Row, 1978), 37.
15. William James, *Varieties of Religious Experience* (New York: New American Library, 1958), 353.
16. Benedicta Ward, *The Desert Christian* (New York: Macmillan, 1975), 242.
17. Rainer Maria Rilke, *Letters to a Young Poet* (New York: W. W. Norton & Co., 1934), 20, 35.

18. Morton Kelsey, *The Other Side of Silence* (New York: Paulist Press, 1976), 84.
19. Martin Buber, *Tales of the Hasidim Early Masters* (New York: Schocken, 1948), 53.
20. Teresa of Avila, *Mansions of the Interior Castle,* as quoted in Kenneth Leech, *Soul Friend* (New York: Harper & Row, 1977), 150.
21. Thomas Corbishly, trans., *The Spiritual Exercises of St. Ignatius Loyola* (Wheathampstead, Hertfordshire: Anthony Clarke, 1973), 12.
22. Leech, *Soul Friend,* 151.

Chapter 2—Biblical Spirituality

1. Nikos Kazantzakis, *The Greek Passion* (New York: Simon & Schuster, 1953), 246.
2. Based on a story by Edward Hayes in *The Ethiopian Tattoo Shop* (Easton, Kans.: Forest of Peace Books, 1983), 88–94. By permission.
3. Paul Reps, compiler, *Zen Flesh, Zen Bones* (New York: Doubleday, 1961), 47.
4. Ira Progoff, *The Practice of Process Meditation* (New York: Dialogue House, 1980), 188–89.
5. Shema: The first word in Deuteronomy 6:4 is *shema,* "hear," which became Judaism's affirmation of monotheism. Later it was extended to include verses 5–9; 11:13–21 (blessing for its fulfillment and curse for its neglect); and Numbers 15:37–41. It consists of six words and phrases: 1. Hear; 2. O Israel; 3. Yahweh, Lord; 4. Our God; 5. Yahweh; 6. One. The Shema, or Shem, was recited morning and evening and became the Jewish martyrs' cry through the centuries, the symbol of their faith.
6. Theophane the Monk, *Tales of a Magic Monastery* (New York: Crossroad, 1981), 19.
7. Walter Wangerin, Jr., *Miz Lil and the Chronicles of Grace* (New York: Harper & Row, 1988), 24–25.

Chapter 3—Religious Experience

1. William James, *Varieties of Religious Experience* (New York: Collier Books, 1961), 40.
2. Gregory Bateson, *Mind and Nature* (New York: E. P. Dutton, 1979), 209.
3. Anthony de Mello, *Sadhana, A Way to God* (New York: Doubleday, 1984).
4. Evelyn Underhill, *Mysticism* (New York: New American Library, 1974), 269.
5. Ibid., 282.

6. Charles Williams, *The Greater Trumps* (Grand Rapids: Eerdmans, 1950), 191.
7. Richard F. Vieth, *Holy Power, Human Pain* (Bloomington: Meyer-Stone Books, 1988), 137.
8. Frances G. Wickes, *The Inner World of Choice* (Boston: Sigo Press, 1988), 10.
9. Ibid., 11–19.
10. Ira Progoff, *The Symbolic and the Real* (New York: McGraw-Hill, 1963), 146–53.
11. Dag Hammarskjold, *Markings* (New York: Ballantine, 1964), 180.
12. Ira Progoff, *At a Journal Workshop* (New York: Dialogue House, 1975).
13. C. G. Jung, *Memories, Dreams, Reflections* (New York: Vintage Books, 1965), vi, xii.

Chapter 4—The Story As Spiritual Guide

1. Martin Buber, *Tales of the Hasidim Later Masters* (New York: Schocken, 1948), 251.
2. Joseph Campbell, *The Power of Myth* (New York: Doubleday, 1988), 22.
3. Jim Fowler and Sam Keen, *Life Maps* (Waco, Tex.: Word Books, 1970), 161.
4. Laurens van der Post, *The Heart of the Hunter* (New York: William Morrow and Co., 1961), 172.
5. Reprinted with permission from *St. George and the Dragon and the Holy Quest for the Grail* (Forest of Peace Books, Inc.—Easton, Kans., 66020).
6. C. S. Lewis, *God in the Dock* (Grand Rapids: Eerdmans, 1970).

Chapter 5—Creation Spirituality

1. Yushi Nornura, *Desert Wisdom: Sayings from the Desert Fathers* (Garden City: Doubleday, 1982).
2. Lewis Thomas, *The Medusa and the Snail* (New York: Viking, 1979), 8.
3. Gerard Manley Hopkins, *The Poems of Gerard Manley Hopkins*, eds. W. H. Gardner and N. H. MacKenzie (New York: Oxford University Press, 1967), 66.
4. Annie Dillard, *Pilgrim at Tinker Creek* (New York: Bantam Books, 1982), 279.
5. Hopkins, *Poems*, 66.
6. Edward Robinson, *The Original Vision* (New York: Seabury, 1983), 32.
7. From *If Mountains Die* by John Nichols. Copyright (c) 1979 by John

Nichols and William Davis. Reprinted by permission of Alfred A. Knopf Inc.

8. John M. Rich, *Chief Seattle's Unanswered Challenge* (Fairfield, Wash.: Ye Galleon Press, 1947), 40.

9. Dillard, *Pilgrim*, 16.

10. Anthony de Mello, *The Song of the Bird* (New York: Doubleday, 1984), 170.

11. Thomas Merton, *Conjectures of a Guilty Bystander* (Garden City: Image Books, 1968), 160.

12. Martin Buber, *Tales of the Hasidim Later Masters* (New York: Schocken, 1948), 62.

13. Agnes Sanford, *The Healing Light* (New York: Ballantine Books, 1972), 1.

14. C. S. Lewis, *The Magician's Nephew* (New York: Macmillan, 1955).

15. Cited in Matthew Fox, *Original Blessing* (Santa Fe: Bear & Co., 1984), 70.

16. Merton, *Conjectures*, 12.

17. Rainer Maria Rilke, *Letters to a Young Poet* (New York: W. W. Norton & Co., 1934), 59.

18. Gertrud Mueller Nelson, *To Dance with God* (Mahwah: Paulist Press, 1986), 3.

19. Anne Morrow Lindbergh, *Gift from the Sea* (New York: Vintage, 1978), 106.

20. Charles Williams, *The Greater Trumps* (Grand Rapids: Eerdmans, 1950), 74.

Chapter 6—Prophetic Spirituality

1. Antoine de Saint-Exupery, *The Little Prince* (New York: Harcourt Brace Jovanovich, 1971), 84.

2. Francis MacNutt, *Healing* (Notre Dame: Ave Maria Press, 1985), 34.

3. Tilda Norberg and Robert Webber, *Stretch Out Your Hand* (New York: United Church Press, 1990). In press.

4. Ernst Kasemann, *Jesus Means Freedom* (Philadelphia: Fortress Press, 1968), 16.

5. Matthew Fox, *On Becoming a Musical Mystical Bear* (New York: Paulist Press, 1976), 110.

6. Thomas Merton, trans. *The Wisdom of the Desert: Songs from the Desert Fathers of the Fourth Century* (New York: New Directions, 1960), 51.

7. Allan Boesak, *Black and Reformed* (Maryknoll: Orbis Books, 1984), 45.

8. Julian of Norwich, *Showings* (New York: Paulist Press, 1978), 225.

9. Norberg and Webber, *Stretch*.

10. Anonymous, *The Cloud of Unknowing and Other Works*, trans. Clifton Wolters (New York: Viking Penguin, 1978), 83–91.
11. Bruce Ritter, *Sometimes God Has a Kid's Face* (New York: Covenant House, 1988), 82–3.

Bibliography

Anonymous. *The Cloud of Unknowing and Other Works,* trans. Clifton Wolters. New York: Viking Penguin, 1978.

Barry, William A., and William J. Connolly. *The Practice of Spiritual Direction.* New York: Seabury Press, 1982.

Bartholomew, Gilbert L. "Nicodemus, a Dialog in the Style of a Current Genre and Drawing on Traditional Sayings of Jesus," paper distributed to class. Lancaster, Pa.: Lancaster Theological Seminary, 1987.

Brown, Raymond E. *The Gospel According to John I-XII.* The Anchor Bible Series. New York: Doubleday, 1966.

Caprio, Betsy. *The Woman Sealed in the Tower: A Psychological Approach to Feminine Spirituality.* New York: Paulist Press, 1982.

de Mello, Anthony. *Sadhana.* New York: Doubleday, 1984.

———. *The Song of the Bird.* New York: Doubleday, 1984.

Edwards, Tildon. *Living in the Presence.* San Francisco: Harper & Row, 1987.

———. *Sabbath Time.* New York: Seabury Press, 1982.

Foster, Richard J. *Celebration of Discipline.* San Francisco: Harper & Row, 1978.

Fowler, Jim, & Sam Keen. *Life Maps.* Waco: Word Books, 1980.

Fox, Matthew. *On Becoming a Musical Mystical Bear.* New York: Paulist Press, 1976.

Fromm, Erich. *The Forgotten Language.* New York: Rinehart & Co., 1951.

Ignatius of Loyola. *The Spiritual Exercises.* Wheathampstead, Hertfordshire: Anthony Clarke, 1987.

James, William. *Varieties of Religious Experience.* New York: New American Library, 1958.

John of the Cross. *Dark Night of the Soul.* Garden City, New York: Image Books, 1959.

Kelsey, Morton T. *The Other Side of Silence.* New York: Paulist Press, 1976.

Leech, Kenneth. *Soul Friend.* San Francisco: Harper & Row, 1977.

Lindars, Barnabas. *The Gospel of John.* The New Century Bible Commentary. Grand Rapids: Eerdmans, 1972.

Maloney, George A. *Prayer of the Heart.* Notre Dame: Ave Maria, 1981.

Merton, Thomas. *Contemplative Prayer.* Garden City: Image Books, 1971.

————. *Conjectures of a Guilty Bystander.* Garden City: Image Books, 1968.

————. *The Wisdom of the Desert: Songs from the Desert Fathers of the Fourth Century.* New York: New Directions, 1960.

Murphy, Miriam. *Prayer in Action.* Nashville: Abingdon, 1979.

Norberg, Tilda, and Robert Webber. *Stretch Out Your Hand.* New York: United Church Press, 1990.

Nouwen, Henri, J. M. *The Way of the Heart.* New York: Ballantine, 1981.

Palmer, Parker. *To Know As We Are Known: A Spirituality of Education.* San Francisco: Harper & Row, 1983.

Progoff, Ira. *The Practice of Process Meditation.* New York: Dialogue House, 1980.

————. *At a Journal Workshop.* New York: Dialogue House, 1975.

Rilke, Ranier Maria. *Letters to a Young Poet.* New York: W. W. Norton & Co., 1934.

Robinson, Edward. *The Original Vision: A Study of the Religious Experience of Children.* New York: Seabury Press, 1983.

Sanford, Agnes. *The Healing Light.* New York: Ballantine, 1983.

Sanford, John A. *Dreams.* New York: Crossroad, 1987.

Sloyan, Gerard. *John: A Bible Commentary for Teaching and Preaching.* Atlanta: John Knox Press, 1988.

Stahl, Carolyn. *Opening to God: Guided Imagery Meditation on Scripture.* Nashville: The Upper Room, 1977.

Thornton, Martin. *English Spirituality.* Cambridge, Mass: Cowley, 1986.

Underhill, Evelyn. *Mysticism.* New York: New American Library, 1974.

Bread for the Banquet

Experiencing Life in the Spirit

Leader's Guide

Elaine M. Ward
A Kaleidoscope Series Resource

United Church Press
New York

Leading This Course

Having agreed to lead this course, you may be experienced in praying, but there will be those in the group you lead who have never learned to pray, those who do not believe in prayer, those who are seeking life in the Spirit, and those who have arrived at spiritual understanding. Your acceptance of persons' deep and diverse feelings will set a tone of openness, for God works in surprising and mysterious ways, and people do change.

For the class area prepare an ambience of quiet, so that the session is a time for participants to come "inside," away from noises, words, and busy confusion, to a place of gentle quietness, quest, and study. Your relaxed manner and tone of voice, unhurried schedule, and openness to doubts and questions will set a mood of calm acceptance, as you lead the group into the presence of God.

The course is designed for six two-hour group meetings, but it can also be used as twelve one-hour sessions. It could be used for retreat groups, Sunday church school sessions, prayer groups, or even for individuals. Choose the material to use with a group on the basis of its needs and interests.

The theme of this study is that God feeds us in many different ways, because of our different tastes and temperaments. Therefore, on the basis of your class's interests, you may want to spend more time with one activity and eliminate others.

You will need a chalkboard and chalk or an easel with newsprint and markers, and a VCR-VHS system for viewing the videotape that accompanies the course. Obtain the videotape early enough for the person who will operate the system to become familiar with it. Make sure that the persons in the course read the first chapter before your first meeting.

Methods of Prayer

Different ways of praying and meditating are suggested in the course to provide for people of a variety of tastes, but the methods should never do harm to individuality. The result is what matters.

Participants must pray as they can, not as they cannot. The interior encounter with God is an encounter with love. Be willing as a group to experiment, to grow, and to change. "Test the spirits" of change by asking whether you and the class are growing in love. Are you less judgmental, more patient, more humble, forgiving of enemies, accepting of self?

Chapter 1: Christian Spirituality

Objectives:
1. To recognize our longing for God.
2. To stimulate and explore questions and doubts about our experiences with prayer and about God's activity, presence, and feeding in our lives and the lives of others.
3. To participate in prayer through silence.

Before class. Set up the VCR and do a practice run for the first session. Have available name tags; paper; pencils; newsprint, markers, and masking tape, or a chalkboard, chalk, and eraser; and the study questions for chapter 2 (see "Questions for Chapter 2" below). When people arrive, greet them, ask them to make out a name tag, and distribute handouts with the following questions:

1. My name is . . .
2. I am here because . . .
3. What I want from this class is . . .
4. I pray (do not pray) because . . .
5. I am most likely to pray when . . .
6. I need God's grace in the following area . . .
7. God feeds me through . . .
8. My question about prayer is . . .

Suggested Process:
Read Isaiah 64:8, and sing "Have Thine Own Way, Lord" or a hymn of your choice. Begin to pray with these words: "Lord, teach us to pray. Hear now our words of silent meditation," and pray in silence. End with the Lord's Prayer or prayers from the group.

Introductions. (a) Introduce yourself as leader; give an experience from your life of prayer. (b) Invite the group to introduce themselves by name and to tell what they hope to receive from this course, or why they are here. (c) *The Video Segment*. View the video's introduction, overview, and the story "A Longing for God," asking the group to be open to what the story says to them as they watch.

After you turn off the video, ask each person to complete the following sentence: "This story says to me . . ." Continue to discuss in small groups of three or four by asking, "What has fed or feeds you?" and "How are people fed spiritually?" Remind the group that "open" questions such as these have no one right answer. Then ask each person to complete the sentence "I long for God because . . ." or "I am hungry for . . ."

Tell or read the story "The Great Banquet" from Luke 14:15–24. Discuss it in the historical setting, as well as the excuses we make today for refusing to "be with God."

Meditate in silence. Ask the participants of the group to sit comfortably, with both feet flat on the floor, eyes closed and hands in lap, and to breathe slowly as follows: take in a deep breath to the count of four and slowly exhale to the count of four. Suggest: "Breathe out thoughts, worries, concerns. Breathe in silence." Some people meditate better with the lights dimmed or out. Say: "Imagine yourself surrounded by thick, soft silence. You are in a cloud of silence inside and out. Swallow the silence. Feel it coat your inner cavities and cover your skin." Sit in silence for five to ten minutes and then ask the group to write whatever they like about the experience as accurately and honestly as possible.

Share their reflections by saying: "How did you attempt to become silent? Describe the silence. What did you experience in the silence? What did you feel or think?" Advise persons not to be discouraged if they did not become silent, for silence is foreign to most people and requires practice. Assure them that with time they will discover the ability to go into deep relaxation immediately.

Read Matthew 6:6–8, and seek silence for another five minutes.

Closing:
Join hands in a circle and close with a brief prayer for protection, strength, and guidance.

Looking Ahead: Assign chapter 2 of the study book and the following questions (duplicated in advance):

Questions for Chapter 2:
1. Ponder what scriptural words have special meaning for you and why. What stories have influenced your trust in God? What stories have "fed" you? Think of a time of crisis, loss, or transition when God fed you. Will you share this with the class?
2. Observe God's "feedings" through the week: Be open to God's love through people, readings, dreams, and other surprises.
3. Read the story "The Board Meeting," in chapter 2 and use it for a meditation.
4. Bring yourself daily into the presence of God through prayer.
5. Invite people to bring a coffee cake and its recipe to the next class as a way of celebrating eating together at the banquet of life.

Chapter 2: Biblical Spirituality

Make copies of Psalm 23 or have Bibles available; also, bring paper and pens, magazines, and newspapers. Have a question box in which the participants may place any questions to be discussed. There is enough material in this session to allow you to choose what will be most meaningful to your group. Spend all the time you need on whatever you choose rather than using all of the material.

Objectives:
1. To pray using the Bible.
2. To encounter some of the biblical stories that feed the spirit and influence daily Christian living.
3. To discuss the biblical understanding of the Holy Spirit.
4. To share favorite scripture verses and stories that have guided, changed, and fed people.
As People Come: Enjoy the fellowship of eating the "breads" together.

Suggested Process:
Read Romans 8:11–19, sing "O Word of God Incarnate," and sing or read aloud "Bread of Heaven."

The Video Segment: Ask persons as they watch video segment 2A, the interviews, to recall their own favorite biblical verses or stories, those that have been influential in feeding, guiding, or changing them into new beings in Christ. After viewing the video segment ask if they are willing to tell how their own lives changed. Discuss: "How does God feed us through scripture? What does the Bible say about God's feedings? What has been the power or purpose of scripture in your life? How does the Bible bring us to wholeness?" In a "popcorn-like" fashion persons can respond to the phrase "The Bible is . . ." Write their responses on the board.

Pray together with scripture:

a. Invite no more than seven persons and no fewer than two to sit close together in a circle. Distribute copies of Psalm 23.

b. Designate a leader.

c. Celebrate the presence of Christ in the promise of Jesus to be with two or three gathered together in his name.

d. The leader reads the psalm aloud, inviting hearers to notice how God's word touches them.

e. Everyone shares the meanings, feelings, thoughts, and images that arise without discussing them.

f. Everyone is silent.

g. The leader repeats the psalm; everyone again shares and then is silent.

h. The leader reads the psalm yet one more time.

i. Everyone prays from the heart and closes with a unison prayer or the singing of a hymn.

The psalmist saw God as shepherd. Ask participants to write their personal metaphors for God, such as teacher, healer, parent, and then to say what the words mean to them by paraphrasing Psalm 23, being faithful to the meaning and message of the text. For instance, "The Lord is my" [insert the metaphor from above] and continue.

The Video Segment: View video segment 2B ("The Board Meeting"). After viewing the segment turn off the video and sit in silence with the words, "Will you, my beloved, will you go?" Ask: Where is it that you are going now? Where do you want to go? Where is God calling you to go?

Ask the group to discuss with a partner or in a small group the meaning of the story for them. Then write an ACTS Prayer

(Adore, Confess, Thank, Supplicate) related to the story by following this format:

A. Begin with praise and love as you come into the presence of your Lord. Ask that the Holy Spirit guide, strengthen, and enlighten you, and say, "Because of this story, I adore you, God, for . . ."

C. Confess those things you have done or have not done that have hurt others or separated you from God, and celebrate God's unconditional love by hearing Jesus say to you, "I know that, and I love you." Then say, "I confess that . . ."

T. Thank God for a specific gift or blessing of the past day. Speak with Jesus with your "faith imagination," being honest about your feelings, and dialogue with him about your concerns. Then say, "And I thank you . . ."

S. Ask God for the grace you need for the living of today, and stay with God in silence. Experience God's presence in your breathing, emptying your mind and enjoying God's love.

Closing:
Ask volunteers to pray aloud, using some part of their ACTS prayer.

Close with a benediction.

Chapter 3: Religious Experience

Objectives:
1. To discuss varieties of religious experience and their meaning.
2. To be open to the power of faith imagination as a way of discerning God's presence and love.
3. To relate dreams to life in the spirit.
4. To experience journal writing as a way of growing spiritually.
As People Come. Invite the group into silence.

Suggested Process:
Slowly read aloud 1 Corinthians 12:4–13, the variety of gifts and work we are given. Brainstorm by asking the group to call out some of their gifts. Together, discuss the variety of religious

experiences and the different breads we are fed at the banquet. List these on the board.

The Video Segment: View video segment 3 on the importance of the use of the imagination and listen to the directions for guided meditation. Read Matthew 13:44–46, and invite participants to do a guided faith meditation. Say: "Be comfortable in your chair with your feet flat on the floor, your hands in your lap, and your eyes closed. Take three deep, slow breaths. Imagine yourselves walking in a meadow. Observe the colors and scents of the flowers. Feel the warm sun soothing your back and arms. Be at peace in the presence of God. [Pause] You experience great joy with a sense that this is the way life was meant to be . . . except for your dream. If only you had your treasure, you would be completely content. Picture that treasure now. Plan steps to obtain it and ask for any help you need. [Pause] Suddenly you notice something. It is a treasure cask lying half buried in the field. You stoop down and look at it and are surprised by what it is, because you believe it is your desire. Feel that joy now. [Pause] Jesus comes into the field. Excitedly you show it to him, telling him what you hope will be inside. Jesus asks you whether that is really what you want. 'Is that your true treasure?' he asks. [Pause] Then he says, 'The kingdom of heaven is like a treasure buried in a field. The one who found it, buried it again and, for sheer joy, went and sold everything he had, and bought that field.' Will you give up all you have for this treasure? [Pause] Take as much time as you need to decide. Listen to your head. Listen to your feelings. Ask, 'Will this help me on my spiritual journey?' [Pause] You may bury the treasure again and return later to purchase the field and the treasure; you may leave it there for someone else to find; or you may take it back with you now. The choice is yours. You are aware that your decision will call for sacrifice and hard work on your part. You may even have to give up all that you now have to possess the treasure. Ask Jesus to help you make your decision. [Pause] After listening to Jesus, decide what you are going to do. When you are finished, open your eyes and return to this place."

Set up feedback with partners. Ask the partners to share their answers to these questions: Were you surprised by what you found? How did you feel when you found it? Why did you or why didn't you sell all you had in order to buy the treasure? Do you have an image for your treasure? If you are willing to share what your treasure is, tell the other person about it now.

If your group would like to create and dramatize a contemporary story based on the pearl of great price, divide into groups of four or five. Give each group a small paper bag with a pearl, a Bible, a map, paper and pencil, and a blank check. Ask them to read again Matthew 13:45–46 and dramatize it by using the items in the bag. Set a time limit; then assemble the entire group to share the stories.

As an introduction to journal writing, invite your group to close their eyes, sit in silence with pen and paper, and list eight to ten significant events in their life in the Spirit. Beside each event, they are to write the supportive person(s) who influenced them spiritually. Ask them to choose one of the events and to write "It was a time when . . ." writing their feelings, dreams, pathways chosen and not chosen, people in their life or work, images of God, and ways in which God seemed to speak to them.

As people conclude their journalizing, ask them to write a prayer discipline for themselves about the when, where, and what (such as using psalms, reading, silence, music, nature, worship, stories, etc.) of prayer, which they would like to try out. For the upcoming week, encourage journalizing each day or at the end of the week. They may want to choose someone with whom to share what they have written, a support person in this discipline.

Closing:
Close with sentence prayers, the Lord's Prayer, and a benediction.

Chapter 4: The Story as Spiritual Guide

Objectives:
1. To experience the power of the story to ignite the imagination and feed the spirit.
2. To hear stories that may reveal God's presence, plan, and promise.
3. To share and explore the meaning of a quest.

Suggested Process:

Sing together "I Love to Tell the Story," or another hymn.

The Video Segment: Introduce the purpose and power of the story by inviting people to listen to the story "God's Secrets," segment 4A, in order to discuss it with a partner. Write the following questions for discussion on a board or chart: How is God revealed? How do you know God? What has God revealed to you?

In small groups of no more than four discuss the story of George's quest in chapter 4, using your own questions, such as: Have you ever been on a quest? What kind of quest was it? What were the reactions of your family and friends? Whom did you meet on your way? Explain the closing words of the story, "You are the Holy Grail."

Discuss with the participants stories as parables, myths, and metaphors. Ask the class to write a metaphor for the kingdom of God. First, think of the things Jesus used to compare to or picture the kingdom, such as the mustard seed that represents God's rule, or the leaven (Matthew 13:31–33). Think of someone whose wages may be small but whose task is big. Think of a quality in your life that is small and in need of growing, or an object that is small but as essential as leaven in the baking of bread, or a part of your body you take for granted but is of great value. Remind participants that love, joy, and trust permeate everything we say or do, as does the leaven of which Jesus spoke. What quality would you like to "grow" in your life (such as patience, imagination, joy, love, hope, trust)?

Lead the class in relaxed imagination: "Sit in a comfortable position and relax. With feet on the floor, head up, and eyes closed, take three deep breaths. Visualize a bowl of yeast dough. Cover it and watch it rise. Of what does it remind you? (The need for waiting? a baby growing? Jesus coming? desire delayed?) Bake it. Let it cool. Enjoy eating it, being filled with its nourishment. Recall a quality you would like to develop. Remember a time when you experienced and tasted that quality in your life. Experience it now. [Long pause] Let it work in you as the yeast in the dough. Go through your day in your imagination, permeating everything with this quality. When you are ready, open your eyes."

The Video Segment: View segment 4B and discuss all or one of the stories by using the following questions:

"Truth and Parable": What did this story say to you? State a truth dressed in parable. What was Jesus' definition of truth? What are the truths by which you live? Does everyone experience truth in the same way? How do stories help a person see truth?

"Careless": Have you ever been careless and then asked Jesus for help? Sit in silence now and pray for discernment (see steps in chapter 6).

"Best Place to Pray": Relate this story to St. George's story about finding a place to pray, making decisions, and committing yourself.

Closing: Using the ACTS prayer from session 2, write or discuss with a partner what God is doing or saying in one of the stories from the video, something that causes you to adore God at this moment. What does it say to you that leads you to confess, be thankful, and entreat God humbly?

Chapter 5: Creation Spirituality

Objectives:
1. To activate an awareness of the Earth's need for peoples' concern and care today.
2. To celebrate the glory of God's creation.
3. To appreciate the unity of body and spirit, and to pray for its feeding and for the unity of all creation.

Suggested Process:
When everyone has gathered, open with prayer.

The Video Segment: View segment 5, a visual essay about peace and wonder through scenes of creation and words of praise. After hearing the poem "Unless," discuss with the group what can be done to conserve natural resources.

Read aloud the poem "If Mountains Die," in chapter 5. Then use Psalm 148 as a choral reading, with one group reading the even verses, a second group reading the odd verses, and both groups reading together verses 13 and 14—a hymn of praise.

Read or tell "The Samaritan Woman," in chapter 5. Then lead the group to meditate in order to hear Jesus for yourselves. Tell them to think of some part of their body or some relationship that they would like to have made whole and healthy. Then say: "Sit quietly, feet on the floor, hands in lap, and take three slow, deep breaths. Allow the tensions and tiredness to flow out of your body. Then imagine yourself walking along a crowded city street in the summer. It is hot. You feel yourself moving, being pushed and jostled by the crowd of people. Get a sense of the heat from the city street and the bodies close around you. Be aware of the smells of the city. Notice the people and discover who is with you. Become aware of your feelings. [Pause] You are becoming very thirsty, but you cannot get out of the crowd. There is nowhere to stop and nothing to drink. Your mouth is dry and you are hot. You keep walking, and as you walk, the crowd disappears so that you are alone. At last you see a well ahead and run to it, eager to drink. But there is no cup and the well is deep. [Pause] Someone comes to help you. (Feel free to bring in anyone you want who will help you get the water.) They have a bucket and a cup, and they give you a drink. You drink, but the dram is bitter and does not quench your thirst. Then Jesus appears saying, 'Anyone who drinks this water will be thirsty again, but anyone who drinks the water that I give will never be thirsty; the water that I give will become a spring of water within, bubbling up for eternal life.' [Pause] You ponder these words and then take the water Jesus offers you. Drink it slowly and feel it flow through your body, refreshing you, renewing you. Feel the cool water in your throat, your chest, your arms and hands and fingers, relaxing you. The water flows into your stomach and then into your legs and feet and toes, renewing all of you. Talk to Jesus about the water he has given you. [Pause] When you are finished, think of somone with whom you wish to share the water, someone who needs Christ's living water. Take the water to the person and tell her or him why you are sharing it. [Pause] When you are finished, say good-bye, knowing you can return. When you feel ready, become aware of where you are, give thanks for water, and open your eyes."

Lead the class in passing the peace by standing, shaking hands or hugging, and granting the "peace of Christ be with you."

In small groups of four or five, discuss the difference between prayer with the head and prayer with the heart and body. Ask the group to state the themes in the chapter that had most meaning to them. As the discussion winds down, state that breathing is important in meditation. In it you will find comfort and guidance. Introduce the "Breathing Prayer" as follows:

Sit quietly with your hands in your lap and your eyes closed. Become relaxed.

1. Become aware of the air as you breathe in and out, as the air passes through your nostrils. Each time you breathe in, think of breathing in God's love and power and peace. Stay with this awareness as long as you can. Breathe in God's divine energy. Breathe out your tensions, fears, and doubts.

2. Be aware of your breathing but do not change it. Simply observe it.

3. Whenever you are distracted, return to your breath observation. Resolve not to miss being aware of a single breath.

4. Become aware of the accompanying calmness and relaxation.

5. Relax your muscles. Picture your whole body filled with light. Let the illuminating light spread to surround you within and without, and if you choose to pray for someone, surround that person with the radiance of that light of God's love.

6. Become aware of the coldness of the air as it comes in and of its warmth as it leaves.

7. Stay with the breathing awareness for ten or fifteen minutes. Sing "Breathe on Me, Breath of God."

Pray with Nature. To experience the connectedness of all things, lead the group in the following meditation. Look at a seashell or a leaf for ten minutes. Observe each line flowing into the other, extending from the center. Turn to awareness of the breath, return to observation of the object. Alternate. As a variation, choose a word or image related to nature, such as fire, water, sun, Earth, etc. Contemplate the associations as they arise. Then become aware again of the breath. Finally, after you have done the above a few times, pay attention to a problem related to creation. Present the problem as a word or image and proceed as above, keeping open and expectant but without particular expectations. Always return to simple awareness of the breath. Encourage the class to not think about the images or problems, but to simply hold them in their awareness.

Sing "Guide Me, O Thou Great Jehovah," calling attention to the words "Bread of heaven, feed me till I want no more."

Closing:

Read the story of Ali at the end of chapter 5 and pray: "Dear Master, Creator, help us unblock our own polluted streams; help us remove the garbage we have accumulated in the materialistic, product-oriented, technological time we have spent here on your planet. Burn away the dross of desire, except that for your presence. Help us exchange our values for Christ's values. In the name of the One who taught us to love. Amen."

Looking Ahead:

The next session will include a simple communion service. You or a member of your group will need to bring one or several loaves of bread, a cup, and wine or grape juice.

Chapter 6: Prophetic Spirituality

Objectives:

1. To relate life in the spirit to prophetic spirituality.
2. To attempt to discern God's will in our lives.
3. To experience Christ's presence in Holy Communion.

Suggested Process:

Pray, and sing "Awake, Awake to Love and Work" or "For the Bread Which Thou Hast Broken."

Read aloud Luke 10:38–42 and reflect as a group on the meaning of the story.

Ask each group member to discuss with a partner these questions: On a scale of one to ten how is your church feeding you? How is it nurturing your spiritual growth? your prophetic spirituality? How do you feed in your church? What suggestions do you have for your church's feeding of yourself and others? What would you like to change? Rate your church's and your own involvment in prophetic spirituality. What is your model for work in the world? How does life in the spirit relate to prophetic spirituality? Allow time for the group to discuss this theme as it is developed in chapter 6.

Guide the group in this meditation: "In the last story of John's Gospel, after the resurrection, Jesus came to his friends in the dark, in the early morning, on the shore. I invite you to close your eyes and, in the darkness, use your imagination to be on the shore now, where you too may meet Jesus. In the silence, breathe in the breath of life, breathe out your tensions and troubles. Feel yourself walking along the shore of a lake. It is early morning and still dark. You can hear the water gently rolling over the sandy shore, in and out, reminding you of the ebb and flow of life itself. [Speak slowly] You feel the wet sea mist sweep over your face. You hear the seagulls crying and smell fish frying. You look in the direction of the aroma and see Jesus calling you to come eat with him. You run toward him, for you know your need for bread and fish. He takes the bread and gives it to you and does the same with the fish. You eat. It is good to fill an empty stomach. You relax in Jesus' presence. It is good to fill an empty spirit. In the darkness Jesus whispers, 'Do you love me more than these? Do you love me more than any other person?' [Pause] You shake your head. With food still in your mouth, you mumble, 'Yes, Lord, you know that I love you.'

"'Feed my lambs.' Take time to picture what this means to you. Whom can you feed? In what way? Jesus speaks the question again. This time in a loud, firm voice, 'Do you love me more than possessions or success?'

"'Yes, Lord, you know that I love you.'

"'Take care of my sheep!' What will you need to let go in order to feed Christ's sheep? Suddenly Jesus stands up and shouts, 'Do you love me more than your own life?' You answer in your own words, remembering the many times you have denied him, and you think on what God wants *you* to do. [Pause] 'Feed my sheep!' [Pause] And when you are ready, open your eyes, return to this place."

The Video Segment: View segment 6A, recalling the need for the eucharist and worship to feed the community in order that they can go out into the world to feed others. Share stories of special experiences of the sacrament of communion.

Divide into groups of four, each group sitting around a loaf of bread. Say to the group, "Observe the bread and let it have its effect on you. How does God love you and feed you through the bread? Silently dialogue with the bread in your imagination, saying 'From where did you come? What do you mean to me? Of what or whom are you a symbol? What do I do with you?'"

Sing "Kum Ba Ya" or "Let Us Break Bread Together."

Read Isaiah 58:6–10 aloud, and stand in a circle to pass the loaf, each person holding the bread for the person to their left, saying as he or she takes it, "This is the body of Christ to reconcile the world. Feed my sheep," and the cup, "This is the blood of Christ to reconcile the world. Feed my sheep."

The Video Segment: View segment 6B and discuss it by asking: "How is prophetic spirituality related to prayer and 'bread for the banquet'?"

If there is time, ask participants to write their prayers of confession or thanksgiving. Or distribute newspapers for the group to scan for news and headlines that relate to prophetic spirituality. Cut them out and paste them on paper, allowing for room to write above, beside, or under such biblical verses as Luke 4:16–19; Matthew 25:34–40; Psalm 82:3–5; 85:11–12; Isaiah 45:22–25; 58:6; and a verse from Isaiah 51 or 52.

Closing:

Use intercessory prayers for the world.